THE LAND ROVER EXPERIENCE

A user's guide to four-wheel driving

Tom Sheppard

Published by

This book deals with post-1986 model Land Rovers, Defenders, Discoverys and Range Rovers where details of controls and transmission are concerned. The vast majority of the book's advice and philosophy, however, may be applied to all Land Rover operations with appropriate discretion.

Published by
Land Rover and G T Foulis and Company, part of the Haynes Publishing Group
Project conceived and directed at Land Rover by Roger Crathorne .
Written, designed and produced for Land Rover by Tom Sheppard, MBE, ARPS.
Illustration artwork by Mike Lister of Plum Advertising, London.
© Tom Sheppard 199 3

Photography
Land Rover: Jacket upper rt, pp 3, 4, 11 rt, 21 rt, 23 lt, 27, 33 rt, 41 rt, 43 lt, 44 rt, 59 rt, 64 lt, 71 rt, 72, 73, 75, 103, 122, 123, 128. Mike Hallett: p 87 lt. Superwinch: p 89 top. Jardine PR: p 122 top.
All remaining photography: Tom Sheppard.

Acknowledgements
The author would like to express grateful thanks for their interest, help, and enormous patience to:
David Bowyer, Bradley Doublelock (Philip Hanson), Commercial Body Fittings (Mick Bowling), Dubai Equestrian Centre (Dervilla Campbell), Fortune Promoseven (Donal Kilalea, Jihad el Sibai), Fresh Tracks (Daniel Collins), Ib Kidde-Hansen, Marlow Ropes (Andy Street), Michelin Tyres (Terry Khokhar), Paul O'Connor, Geoff Renner, Tom Robson, Tarmac Roadstone (Andrew McGarva), Daruish Zandi.
And within Land Rover: Chris Batiste, Tony Bourne, John Carter, Roger Crathorne, Neil Dodswell Dave Drummond, David Fulker, Alison Grose, Mike Gould, Kate Higton, Colin Hill, Chris Hoyle, Roger Hughes, Phil Jones, Tony Northway, Adam Ormandy, Colin Parkes, David Saunders, Chris Scaife, Harry Turnbull, Russell Turnham

Land Rover Experience

CONTENTS

...continued

SECTION 4. OPERATIONS – THE DETAILS 37

SECTION 5. OPERATIONS – RECOVERY 77

SECTION 6. ADVANCED DRIVING 93

...continued

SECTION 7. DATA

Land Rover Experience

Introduction

Who this book is for. If you have recently acquired your first Land Rover product – or even your first four-wheel drive vehicle – we hope you will find this book useful in understanding and getting the best out of it. Even if you have been operating 4x4s for some time – a single vehicle or a fleet–there may still be some tips that will help you and your colleagues to use your vehicles more effectively, more safely and more durably – the key to successful fleet operation.

Aim. The aim of the techniques outlined in this book is to realise the fullest potential of your Land Rover product, to make your driving as safe and relaxed as possible, to ensure that in difficult conditions you get stuck as infrequently as possible, to ensure you hazard your vehicle as little as possible and that you damage it not at all. It makes sense to mention the rationale behind the advice and for this reason safety is emphasised throughout.

Short term use. Use this book like a tiny encyclopaedia. Use the index, glossary, contents pages, section headings and side-notes to go straight to whatever is your current query. Cross-referencing and a degree of repetition in the book will enable you to do this quickly.

Long term use. You will not carry all of this book in your head. But as you peruse it you will absorb the principles needed to become a sensitive and (therefore) proficient off-road driver. You will not only get to know the strengths and limitations of your vehicle but you will get to know how to read the ground and apply the variations of technique you will encounter. Soon it will all come instinctively; you will have written your own book.

Manual and automatic transmission. Many off-road commercial operators tend to favour manual transmissions, often for reasons of initial cost and commonality with earlier fleet vehicles. Because manual transmissions require more detailed description, the emphasis in this book should not be interpreted as favouring that technology. Automatic transmission has considerable advantages and, used on- or off-road, is very operator-friendly.

Additive experience. Many readers will already have experience in off-road operation and have developed their own techniques of doing things. We found, in the preparation of this book, that such inputs are always valuable and often apparently conflicting methods did not in fact conflict at all – they were just suited to subtly different sets of conditions. Experience was nearly always additive rather than reflecting opposite techniques; given common aims of safety and care of the vehicle the best course was usually self-evident.

Glossary, index, technical data. Some terms and usages may be new to you and a glossary (p 147) attempts to explain the most basic and the most specialist terms encountered.   The technical data section shows current vehicle specifications which inevitably vary from country to country; space does not permit them all to be shown. Those given are for the UK.

Fragile earth. Far more important than the current fashion that it may seem, we would ask you, in closing, to maintain your vigilance against environmental damage in the operation of your four-wheel drive vehicle. We all share the responsibility. Enjoy your driving!

Land Rover Experience

SECTION 1

FOUR-WHEEL DRIVE – THE INGREDIENTS

WHY FOUR-WHEEL DRIVE

Halving the load

4x4 equals four-by-four equals four-wheel drive.

Terminology. It is worth an initial thought about what four-wheel drive or 4x4 really does do. Incidentally, 4x4, spoken as 'four-by-four' means there are four wheels, of which four are driven by the engine. So a normal car, be it front wheel drive or rear wheel drive, is a 4x2 'four-by-two' – four wheels in total, of which the car is driven by two. Some types of truck are referred to as a 6x4 – six (wheels driven) by four.

What it does – and doesn't do. A 4x4 does not double the power on the road; it takes the power you do have and spreads it between four wheels instead of only two. If a vehicle needs a certain amount of push (tractive effort or traction) to make it go at a given speed or traverse a certain type of terrain, a 4x4, by having twice as many driven wheels as a 4x2, will actually halve the tractive load on a given piece of ground and thus greatly reduce the chance of slipping, skidding or spinning wheels. Four-wheel drive is thus a considerable benefit to effective operation and to safety. If 4x4 is now combined with large wheels and large amounts of wheel movement on supple, well damped springs, the ingredients of an effective off-road vehicle, capable of operating on rough uneven ground, are starting to take shape.

4x4 spreads power between four wheels, reducing risk of slip.

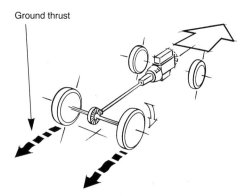

Ground thrust

4x2 – all the power on two wheels. High ground stress. Wheels may slip or spin.

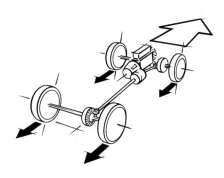

4x4 – same power spread between four wheels. Half the ground stress. Double the traction.

Doubling the effect

Where 4x2s slip a 4x4, demanding less of the ground, will grip.

Maintaining traction. Thus if conditions are such that an ordinary 4x2 car driving only one pair of wheels could spin those wheels and lose traction, a 4x4 will actually be twice as effective in using the power of the engine to maintain traction.

More from four. The diagrams sum up what we have been discussing. All over the world there are bits of ground – oily tarmac, icy roads, glazed snow, wet grassy fields – that will not support the tractive effort needed under certain conditions when power is put through one pair of wheels. Put that power through two axles – four wheels – thus halving the traction

Traction from the wheel at each corner of the vehicle is the overriding advantage of four-wheel drive on roads. Off-road it is even more important.

required of each wheel, and your 4x4 is likely to get you through – securely and under complete control.

Even 4x4s have limits. Of course conditions may be so bad or the traction required so high that even a 4x4 spins its wheels or needs lower gears. These

occasions are addressed later in the book but in general four-wheel drive enhances safety and effectiveness on and off road at all times. As we shall see, if you are driving any of the current Land Rover range and are therefore in four-wheel drive all the time, without having to select it specially, then you are at a further advantage.

4x4 enhances security. Unlike many makes, Land Rover vehicles are in 4x4 all the time.

Land Rover Experience

TRACTION

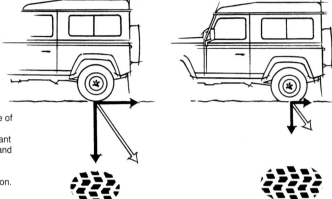

Big footprint (right) results from lowered tyre pressures. For vehicle of given weight and torque, arrows represent weight, thrust and resultant force *per unit area* of tyre contact and therefore per unit area of ground. Less ground stress equals less chance of slip and thus more traction. See also pp 56, 58, 112.

Large wheels, beam axles

Big footprint equals low ground stress equals more traction.

Pushing backwards and downwards. The diagram shows that as well as tractive load pushing backwards on the ground under each wheel there is, of course, also the weight of the vehicle pushing downwards. 4x4s have big wheels and therefore big tyres – which have a bigger 'footprint' than small tyres. Under certain circumstances, although 4x4s are heavier than light cars, a 4x4 tyre can be used at reduced inflation pressures to make an even larger footprint so that, again, the amount of support (and traction) asked of a given piece of ground can be reduced. See diagrams above.

Big wheels: smooth ride, flotation. But lowered tyre pressures, as we shall see later in Section 7 (p 110), are more of an emergency measure. The day-to-day advantages of big wheels and beam axles as used on Land Rover products derive from the fact that the larger the diameter of the wheel, the smoother the ride over rough ground whilst, of course, giving better flotation too.

Big wheels also give smooth ride, maximum ground clearance.

Ground clearance. Big wheels also ensure greater ground clearance over obstacles. Land Rover vehicles' beam axles keep this ground clearance constant – unlike an independently sprung front end on other vehicles – and keep the tyres' tread always flat on the ground. The diagram below shows how.

Performance potential. So again, traction is enhanced: four-wheel drive, big wheels, beam axles. But when the ground is firm and grippy, you've got four-wheel drive and you want more traction still, say for pulling a horse box or a boat or for going up a very steep slope..? That is when you need an extra low bottom gear – see next paragraph.

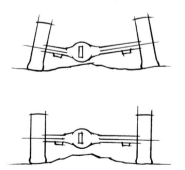

Independently sprung axle (top) loses ground clearance on one-wheel bump. Land Rover's beam axle (below) less liable to lose traction through grounding.

Extra gears

Lower gearing. Extra low gears are just what are available on most 4x4s but not all in the same gearbox. The transfer box on a 4x4 got its name because it is what transfers power from the normal gearbox to the rear axle and front axle thus making it a 4x4. But this extra transfer gearbox is also a two-speed affair with a high ratio and a low ratio. Making a single gearbox with ten forward speeds which could be successively selected would result in an expensive, heavy and complicated item.

Doubling the number of gears. The two-speed transfer box is 'downstream' of the main gearbox and by selecting low ratio it gears-down all the gears in the normal gearbox. In 'high' the gears are unaffected. So your Land Rover has a transfer box to effect the four-wheel drive function and additionally to provide what amounts to a complete set of very low gears.

Low ratio for heavy jobs. The 'low box' is selected for specific heavy duty tasks using a separate lever as we shall see (p 18–21).

All the tricks at once. A Discovery displays the attributes of an off-road 4x4 in a common combination – the gradability (ability to climb steep obstacles) afforded by the low transfer gears, the facility of providing drive to each wheel, the extreme wheel movement – see also p 32 – and the benefits of the one-piece beam-axle.

Traction is power without slip. Big tyres and 4x4 minimise slip; a low ratio transfer box gives the 'power'.

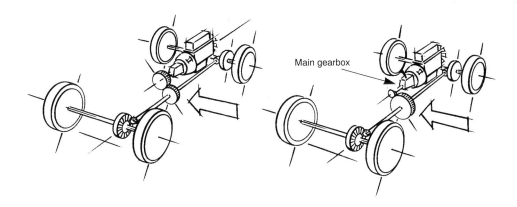

Main gearbox

Concept of transfer box in 1:1 high ratio (left) and low ratio (right) which gears-down the final drive to give more 'power' at the wheels. Note that the main gearbox is 'up-stream' – ie between the engine and the transfer gearbox.

PERMANENT FOUR-WHEEL DRIVE

Why centre differential

Selectable 4x4. On some 4x4s the four-wheel drive function is itself selectable. Normal driving is done in two-wheel drive – as a 4x2 – and the driver has to decide when conditions require 4x4. In such vehicles the front and rear axles, which in fact revolve at slightly different speeds, are locked together when 4x4 is selected without any ability to accommodate the front/rear speed difference. The result is transmission 'wind-up' or tyre-scrub – most usually a combination of both; such vehicles can only be driven in 4x4 off-road where the small speed differences can be accommodated by slight wheel slip; they should not be driven on a hard road with four-wheel drive selected.

Permanent 4x4. Since 1983/84 all Land Rover products have been designed with 'permanent 4x4' – the four-wheel drive function is engaged all the time and the front axle, as well as the rear, is driven. Two-wheel drive is not available. But as we shall see, there need be no wind-up or tyre scrub with your Land Rover vehicle.

Improved security, performance. Land Rover, pioneers of the first 'full-time' 4x4, the Range Rover, believe that the extra security and traction performance that result from permanent 4x4 is well worth the extra engineering involved. Such an arrangement also reduces driver workload and makes security and optimum performance an inherent feature of the vehicle rather than being dependent on driver use of a particular feature as in vehicles with selectable 4x4.

Centre diff – the need. Extra engineering? In the same way as the wheel on the

Permanent 4x4 is better on and off road than 4x2 with selectable 4x4.

Centre differential permits slight front/rear axle speed differences due to turns etc.

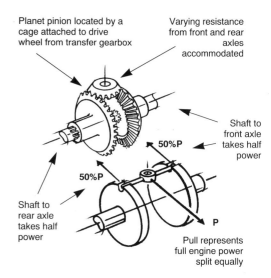

Planet pinion located by a cage attached to drive wheel from transfer gearbox

Varying resistance from front and rear axles accommodated

Shaft to front axle takes half power

50%P

50%P

Shaft to rear axle takes half power

P

Pull represents full engine power split equally

Concept of the centre bevel-type differential that divides engine power between front and rear prop shafts.

outside of a turn travels farther than the wheel on the inside (photo opposite), so the front and rear wheels of a vehicle travel slightly different distances too – again due to the different tracks they follow in bends. So a 4x4 vehicle with permanent four-wheel drive needs a differential arrangement between the front and rear axle drives to accommodate the slight front/rear rotational differences – in the same way as there has been a differential between left and right wheels on the drive axle of just about every car since the turn of the century.

Land Rover vehicles have one. All Land Rover vehicles made since their adoption of permanent four-wheel drive have a centre differential between the front and rear propeller shafts to even-out the drive torque between front and rear axles, preclude transmission wind-up and prevent tyre scrub.

Illustration right shows different track – and distance travelled – by front and rear wheels in a turn; without a centre differential a permanent-4x4 vehicle would encounter tyre scrub, wheel slip or transmission wind-up. Need for <u>locking</u> centre diff is shown in picture above; a Discovery with centre differential deliberately (and incorrectly) left unlocked in demanding off-road conditions. Grip is markedly different front and rear, due to loose soil and weight transference to the rear; this allows front wheels to spin while rear wheels do not rotate.

Why lockable

Centre diff lock. Current Land Rover products not only have full-time four-wheel drive and a centre differential but that differential is also lockable to enhance traction in difficult situations. It will couple automatically on Range Rovers.

Why. The reason for making it lockable – ie the differential action is temporarily put on hold – is that traction conditions are often different front and rear. For example on a very steep slippery slope weight transference to the back axle may off-load the front wheels enough to let them lose grip and spin. Or there may be occasions when the front wheels are on a grippy rock and the rear wheels are on slippery mud. In these conditions locking the centre differential effectively locks the front prop shaft to the rear prop shaft and precludes lost traction through wheel-spin on either axle – see Section 2, p 22.

Where poor grip may permit excessive front/rear axle speed differences, centre differential is locked.

Land Rover Experience

SECTION 2

ENHANCED TRACTION

TRACTION CONTROLS

Transfer lever

Land Rover products have full-time 4x4 plus two-speed transfer box plus centre diff that may be locked.

Traction aids – how and when. As a 'full-time' (ie permanently in) 4x4, a Land Rover vehicle already gives you enhanced traction compared to vehicles driven by one axle only and compared to those with selectable or 'part-time' four-wheel drive. But as we have seen, your Land Rover has additional aids to further enhance its performance – a two-speed transfer gearbox and a lockable centre differential. This section is about how to select these functions and when to use them.

The 'little gear lever'. The small lever adjacent to the gear lever is called the transfer gear lever (since it controls the two-speed transfer gearbox) but you may hear it referred to also as the hi-lo lever or the range change. Its function is to select high range – normal on-road gears – when pulled fully aft, or low range (sometimes referred to as 'low ratio') when pushed fully forward. Normally these selections should be made when the vehicle is stationary or below 8 kph (5 mph) though there may be occasions (see Section 6, p 94) when you may wish to (and can) go from low range to high range on the move.

Transfer lever controls low/high ratio (fore and aft); and (except in post-1988 Range Rovers, see VCU, p 159) engages centre diff-lock when moved to left – in high or low.

Small lever beside main gear lever controls engagement of high or low ratio transfer gears – see diagram p 13. Same lever, moved to left, engages centre differential lock in high or low ratio; on current Range Rover this function is effected by the VCU (p 159). Photos show Defender left, Discovery, Range Rover LSE automatic top right.

Low ratio. The next spread – p 20, 21 – gives detail on when and how the 'low box' should be used.

Diff lock, electronic traction control, handbrake

Fore and aft, side to side. The same lever, as well as moving fore and aft to select low and high ratio, is moved to the left of the gate – in either high or low range positions – to lock the centre differential, the so-called 'diff lock' (see p 14 concerning centre differential and diff lock; see also p 22 for more details on when and how to use diff lock).

Electronic traction control – (ETC). ETC is a feature on current ABS-equipped Range Rovers which inhibits wheel-spin by applying pulsed brake to a spinning rear wheel and thus enhances traction on ice, snow or in severe off-road conditions. Like

Really steep slopes call for all the traction controls – low transfer gears (see next page), centre differential lock (see p 22 and picture p 15), and a readiness to use the parking brake. As diagram shows, handbrake operates on transmission propeller shaft so should not be used when vehicle is moving. On extreme slopes vehicle should also be in gear with diff lock engaged.

ABS, it is especially effective in maintaining control when one side of the vehicle is on a more slippery surface than the other.

Handbrake – only when stationary. As it is adjacent to the transfer gear lever it is worth mentioning the handbrake at this point although it is not strictly speaking a traction control. The handbrake on Land Rover products acts on a drum on the rear propeller shaft immediately aft of the gearbox and as such it is extremely powerful. The handbrake should be regarded as a parking brake only. Use of this handbrake when the vehicle is moving at all will cause severe juddering shock loads and wind-up to the transmission. For this reason, except in emergencies, *the handbrake should never be applied until the vehicle is stationary.* **WARNING. Under no circumstances should you attempt to use it for trying to do 'hand-brake turns'.**

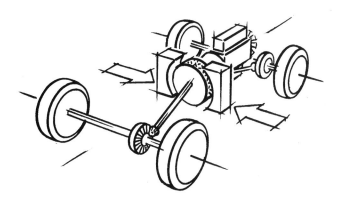

Concept of handbrake shown, with drum on rear propshaft immediately aft of transfer gearbox (in fact, the brake drum has internally-expanding shoes). When centre diff-lock is engaged handbrake effectively works on both prop shafts as they are then locked together.

CAUTION. Handbrake is a transmission brake; do not apply while the vehicle is moving. Use as parking brake only (except in emergency).

LOW RANGE – WHEN AND HOW

'Power' and 'control'

Low range for power. As we have seen, selecting low ratio on the transfer box is not just another gear but affects all the gears in the main gear box (including reverse), gearing them down by nearly 2:1. The obvious uses of the low range are thus occasions when you want a great deal of 'power' or tractive effort – towing a car out of a ditch, ascending a very steep slope, getting out of deep mud or sand, pulling a fallen tree trunk out of the way.

Low ratio gears the vehicle down by nearly 2:1 and provides enormous tractive effort.

Low range for control. Less immediately obvious uses for the low ratio include the provision of *control* rather than high tractive effort. Examples of this might be steadying the vehicle on a very steep descent without use of the brakes or, classically, allowing the vehicle to crawl over rocks slowly, steadily, without jarring and with your foot off the clutch pedal and without use of the brakes. Low box, first gear excels in this kind of exercise and can often be used with minimal throttle opening or even at idling revs.

Low range 1st gear provides superb control for slow, steady crossing of obstacles such as rocks.

Low 1st – too low? Low range first, because of its enormous 'power' capability, is often too low for slippery surface conditions and it is easy for you to spin the wheels inadvertently. It should be used when grip is good, when momentum is not required and when there is little danger of spinning the wheels – or when considerable tractive effort is needed.

What to start off in

For most situations, start in 2nd; 3rd, 4th, 5th are for 'getting around' on rough ground.

Low 2nd – rule-of-thumb. Second is a good rule-of-thumb starting-off gear for most low ratio situations – muddy conditions, steep slopes and the like even

with a heavy trailer. Because tractive effort available is then more closely matched to what the ground will take, there is less risk of wheel spin and the lost traction that results.

Low 3rd, 4th, 5th – versatility. Third, fourth and fifth gears in the low range are good 'getting about' gears for the better parts of derelict mountain or desert tracks, for getting across the field, for forest tracks that are a bit tight for high range. They bring out the vehicle's versatility and the ease with which it traverses cross-country terrain; you can make a respectable speed in fifth, yet change all the way down to second when the going gets more difficult (see Section 4 – 'Driving on tracks', p 42).

Driver still the key. We shall see in the ensuing sections specific examples of what gears to use. And also that there is more to maintaining traction than just selecting a

Saharan boulders epitomise the 'control' case where low range 1st gear gives steady rock-crawling capability. 1st gear start sometimes appropriate to heavy towing but higher gears provide general off-road flexibility (left). Avoid temptation to 'use clutch as another gear'.

low gear; driver sensitivity is half the battle – see Section 3 – 'Gentle right foot', p 28. (See also Section 6 – 'High/low range overlap', p 94 about situations that can be dealt with using high *or* low range.)

Automatic transmission. As in high range, automatic transmission will start the vehicle in first gear and change up as far as it is permitted by the position of the gear selector lever – all the way up to 4th gear if it is in 'D', up to 3rd if the lever is at '3', no higher than 2nd if the lever is at '2', and it will hold 1st if the lever is moved back to '1'. You thus have total control – see also Section 6 , 'Automatic Transmission', p 96.

*Driver sensitivity –
a gentle right foot –
is still the main key.*

CENTRE DIFFERENTIAL LOCK

When to use diff lock

Poor traction overcome. As we have seen, the centre differential may be locked as required or, on Range Rovers, will lock automatically when this action is needed. The reason for the provision of the locking facility on the centre differential which separates the front and rear propeller shafts is that there are a number of poor-traction situations when such a lock will enhance the vehicle's performance. See also Section 1 – 'Permanent four-wheel drive', p 14.

Range Rover's centre diff lock is automatic – actuated by viscous coupling (see glossary p 159).

Spinning wheels. Many will be familiar with the single spinning wheel of a conventional car on an icy road. This is the result of the drive wheels being on surfaces of different grip characteristics – one wheel on ice with the other on dry road. It is possible for the same situation to arise in a 4x4 – front axle on firm, grippy concrete while the rear axle is in mud. An extreme example but you will understand the principle – which applies to a greater or lesser extent in nearly all off-road situations.

On Discovery and Defender, select centre diff lock when there is any risk of losing grip.

When to use diff lock. A simple rule-of-thumb is to use diff lock (see below how) when you use the low box on any loose or slippery surface. Use of the low box generally means that you are on difficult or uneven ground and wanting a high tractive effort. Such ground usually has uneven traction characteristics as well as an uneven surface and, with low box you will be needing all the traction (grip) you can get. Locking the centre differential will preclude loss of traction resulting from potential front/rear differences in grip.

Be sure to de-select diff lock when on a firm, level, non-slippery surface.

High range diff lock? It is possible to engage diff lock in high range too. When, if ever, is this desirable? It will be useful to

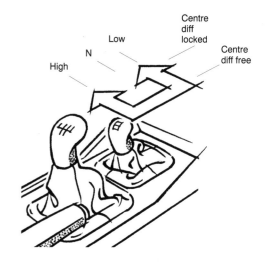

Diagram shows movement of transfer lever to select diff lock. Inset shows warning light – not present on Range Rovers which have automatic diff lock. Poor-traction low-box off-road conditions more effectively tackled with diff lock.

engage diff lock in high range when driving on potentially difficult surfaces such as wet grass, mud, loose or packed snow, or loose sand on tracks or in open desert.

When to de-select diff lock. It is important to *de-select* diff lock (see below how) when on any hard grippy surface such as tarmac or concrete (wet or dry) whether you are in high or low range. The 'DIFF LOCK' warning light will illuminate when the diff is locked and should be a reminder to you. If you do not de-select on grippy surfaces the steering will feel stiff, there will be excessive tyre wear through scuffing and there will be transmission wind-up putting excessive strain on the transmission which may make it hard to use the transfer gearbox lever to disengage low ratio.

Diff lock indicator light

Controls and indicators

How to select and de-select diff lock. On any Land Rover model where diff lock selection is not automatic the transfer lever can move side to side as well as fore and aft; move the transfer lever to the left to select diff lock – whether you are in high or low range. Make it a habit to release pressure on the accelerator momentarily as you do this – in case there is a transitory speed difference between front and rear axles at the moment when you select the inter-axle lock. Move the lever to the right to de-select diff lock; when the diff lock disengages the warning light will extinguish.

Diff lock indicator light actuation. The 'DIFF LOCK' indicator will come on when the diff lock is actually engaged – not just when it has been selected. Similarly it will only extinguish when the diff lock is actually disengaged. If the light is reluctant to go out after de-selecting diff lock some transmission 'wind-up' may be present. Reversing for a short distance and then going forward will usually disengage diff lock and extinguish the light.

Automatic diff lock. All current Range Rovers have viscous coupling unit (VCU) centre diff 'lock' selection for which no indicator light is required. A viscous coupling (see Glossary, p 159) joins the two halves of the centre differential and when relative motion between the two halves – ie the front and rear prop shafts – is sensed, the coupling becomes extremely stiff, effectively locking the differential.

To select diff lock, ease the throttle, move transfer lever to left; move to right to de-select. (Discovery and Defender only.)

Diff lock light comes on only when diff lock actually engaged.

SECTION 3

OPERATIONS – PRELIMINARIES

MIND-SET

Smooth operation, making the vehicle flow over the ground rather than jolt, is an indication of the required mechanical sympathy. Work your vehicle well but take the drama out of your driving.

Mechanical sympathy

Be smooth and gentle with your vehicle. Using the power is not the same as being brutal.

Aim smooth. All machinery responds well to being treated with mechanical sympathy – even a vehicle with a reputation for ruggedness such as the Land Rover. There is more to this than just following maintenance schedules and keeping the oil topped up; that is vital but is not the whole user-interface picture. Smooth driving operation should be the aim.

Be kind. Using the very considerable capabilities of your Land Rover product need not preclude your being kind to it. It is a very tolerant vehicle but clunks in the transmission, prolonged wheel-spinning, misuse of the clutch and harsh treatment of any of the controls, engine or suspension should be avoided. Specifically:

Avoid transmission clonks; let the clutch grip fully when it has to. Kill wheel-spin quickly.

1. Transmission controls. (Gear lever and transfer box lever.) Moderate force and moderate speed is the best way to use these levers – firm and gentle. If it is difficult to engage low range, leave the transfer lever where it is, dip the clutch, engage first gear

and let the clutch up slightly to reposition the gear wheels. Keep the clutch down and try again. Similarly, difficulty engaging first or reverse (or noise in doing so) may be eased by dipping the clutch, quickly engaging a higher gear and then trying again.

2. Riding the clutch. *Don't slip the clutch* and 'use it as another gear'. *Don't 'ride' the clutch* either; by this is meant resting your foot on the pedal with slight pressure so as to be able quickly to disengage it. It is natural enough for a properly cautious or inexperienced driver negotiating a difficult piece of terrain to want to be able to use clutch and brake with the minimum delay but riding the clutch – in effect reducing the pressure of the clutch springs – will encourage clutch slip and cause premature wear. Have the clutch fully engaged and your foot clear of the pedal whenever possible.

3. Wheel-spin. As we shall see in more detail, wheel-spin is lost traction and continued wheel-spin will scoop earth

from under the wheels worsening the situation. It is not good for the transmission either. A fast spinning wheel suddenly getting grip can cause shock loading on the transmission and the possibility of transmission damage.

Pride – learn when to back off

Minimise the drama. Probably the most golden of the rules governing difficult off-road driving is to *admit defeat early and reverse out*. Good off-road driving is achieved with the minimum of drama. Huge water splashes, spinning wheels and flying clods of earth are rarely necessary. Even the best drivers perpetrate these fireworks occasionally if they have misjudged the terrain – and usually feel a little sheepish afterwards.

Back off, try again. When a very steep slippery climb stops your vehicle and the wheels begin to spin, back off at once and try again, possibly with a little more speed and in a higher gear. Holding the vehicle with spinning wheels will cause excessive damage to the ground, will worsen the vehicle's chances of making it up the slope and, in some cases, will cause a vehicle to slew sideways-on to the slope and possibly tip. (See also p 48 and p 51 para 5.)

No wheel-spin! The same goes for stretches of deep mud or sand. If you do not make it through the patch first time and there is any sustained wheel-spin, stop before you bog deeper, reverse out and try again using a different route or different tactics. Do not be too proud to admit that you got it wrong.

If it isn't going to go, reverse out while you can and try again.

Getting through second time is better than having to be towed out on the first.

Land Rover Experience

27

GENTLE RIGHT FOOT

Wheel-spin, electronic traction control (ETC)

Reading the ground. You will have seen that effective use of the low range and your Land Rover vehicle's outstanding capabilities depends a lot on a driver's appreciation of how much traction the ground itself will take without allowing wheel-spin.

Ease off the throttle before you get sustained wheel-spin.

Excessive throttle. As with a car on ice, too much throttle will 'over-torque' the driving wheels and make them spin. With such low gearing in the low ratio gears, the same thing can happen with your Land Rover in slippery conditions. Drivers will quickly develop a delicate throttle foot and learn when the conditions are putting the vehicle on the verge of wheel spin.

Spinning wheels dig. Spinning wheels represent loss of traction, often a loss of directional control as well and, getting literally down to earth, can also result in ground being scooped by the spinning tyres from under the wheel and the vehicle becoming stuck. So there are many good reasons for acquiring a sensitive throttle foot and not choosing too low a gear. Both will avoid wheel-spin and help to maintain traction.

Wheel-spin and brake lock-up: two versions of the same thing – a discontinuity of rolling contact.

Electronic traction control, ETC. As already introduced, on p 18 under 'Traction controls', ETC, when fitted, will monitor, and inhibit, inadvertent wheel spin and considerably assist in maintaining traction under limiting conditions.

Climbing slopes like this requires a very sensitive foot on the throttle. Paradoxically you may find you need to ease off the throttle at the steepest part – where the risk of wheel-spin is greatest.

Slide, cadence braking, ABS

Excessive brake. Wheel-spin represents a discontinuity of rolling contact with the ground – the ground and the periphery of the wheel are not going the same speed, ie in stationary contact with one another. Exactly the same situation arises in the case of excessive braking on slippery ground. One or more wheels lock up and slide over the ground resulting in a discontinuity of rolling contact – the periphery of the wheel and the ground are not going the same speed. In one case the wheel is slipping past the stationary ground; in the other the ground is (relatively) slipping past the stationary wheel.

Same foot, same cure – cadence braking. And again the same cures may be used. Lifting your right foot off the throttle will

Continuous rolling contact. Using throttle or brake, avoid spin or slip. Think of your wheels and the ground as a rack and pinion like this.

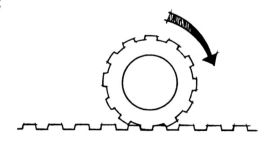

Engine braking's progressive and controllable retardation is best for slopes like these – and almost every other one too. But learn cadence braking for the times when you have got it wrong (top left).

stop wheel-spin and lifting your right foot off the brake will stop wheel slide or skidding. In the case of braking, though, you applied the brakes because you wanted to stop. So re-apply them more gently and, best of all, employ 'cadence braking' technique – repeated jabbing of the brake pedal, quite gently, as fast as you can so that the wheel never gets a chance to lock. Though it takes will power to take your foot off the brakes to do this when you are trying to slow down, cadence braking is remarkably effective.

ABS – automated finesse. It is thus no surprise to find out that the advanced anti-lock brakes (ABS) fitted to the Range Rover Vogue SE and LSE operate on exactly the same principle. They employ a very fast form of cadence braking – you will hear the brake relay working – to obtain the maximum retardation on the most difficult

surfaces, on or off road, without locking up any of the wheels. So in the case of a Range Rover fitted with this feature you will get maximum *available* braking – for given ground conditions – and retain directional control without fear of wheel lock-up.

Engine braking – elegant, gentle. Engine braking, of course, is a very controlled and gentle way to achieve retardation as we shall see in the sections to follow. But even that should not be regarded as an infallible solution to every problem, especially when it is very slippery; you can still finish up with sliding wheels – see Section 6, p 100.

Wheel slide? Back off the brakes and re-apply with repeated gentle jabs.

Engine braking is best for steep down-slopes.

GEOMETRIC LIMITATIONS

Clearance angles

Appreciating clearance. Common to negotiating all types of obstacle off-road is an appreciation of under-body clearance angles, clearance under the chassis and axle differentials and the amount by which the axles can articulate (move up on the near side and down on the off side – and vice versa – see p 32).

Ground clearances, under-chassis angles. It is soon obvious how well all Land Rover products perform cross country but a few moments to study the accompanying diagram will help to refine your judgement on the kind of thing that can and cannot be done without touching bodywork or chassis on the ground. Under-axle clearance is relevant to the size of a single isolated rock on the track that can be driven over but under-belly clearance relates to the (bigger) size of ridge undulations that can be crossed.

Be aware of under-axle clearance – and how it differs from belly clearance.

Ramp angle – belly clearance. The angle measured from the chassis at the centre of the wheelbase down to the periphery of front and rear wheels is the ramp breakover angle, usually called the ramp angle. Its significance is self evident since it governs whether or not you will 'belly' the vehicle on a hump. Such a hump taken fast and without thought of the ramp angle can result in getting stuck with the wheels grappling for traction and the vehicle's weight taken directly on the chassis on the top of the hump – see photo p 80.

Low-set towing hitch can cause tail to dig in on steep ascents or crossing ditches.

Air suspension. A Range Rover fitted with electronic air suspension (EAS – see p 151) has the facility, with 'High profile' selected on the UP button, to increase ride height by 40 mm over standard and, in the process, further improve ramp angle.

Axle clearance. Under-axle clearance is a more obvious limitation. Whilst a Land Rover vehicle running out of axle clearance on soft going will sometimes plough out its own path, do not get into the habit of doing things this way. Deep ruts, rocks submerged in soft mud or encountering hard or rocky going will cause the vehicle to come to a sudden damaging stop when the axle differential housing hits the obstacle.

Approach and departure angles. Approach angles are large on all Land Rover models but remember that tail overhang and

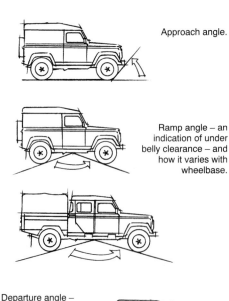

Approach angle.

Ramp angle – an indication of under belly clearance – and how it varies with wheelbase.

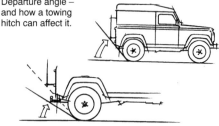

Departure angle – and how a towing hitch can affect it.

Try and develop an awareness, off road, of where parts of the vehicle may touch the ground. The tow hitch (photo right) is the most commonly forgotten. Under-axle and under belly clearances (diagrams) need remembering too.

Under-axle clearance (top) – about 19-23 cm (about 7.5-8.5 in) – is less than under belly clearance. See Section 7 for exact model dimensions.

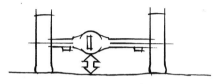

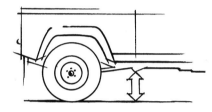

departure angle is the one that will catch you out going up a very steep slope. Regarding the common problem of 'hitting the tail', the departure angle – already less than the approach angle – is further reduced when a low-set towing hitch is fitted and it is not uncommon for an inattentive driver to dig the tow hitch into the ground while going forward up a very steep incline and then find that he cannot

reverse back because the tow hitch prevents him doing so.

Big wheels, short wheelbase. The biggest wheels and the shortest wheelbase will give best under-chassis clearance angles – a Defender 90 on 7.50 x 16 tyres takes the prize. Details of all clearances and geometric limitations for all models and variants are shown at Section 7.

Long wheelbase and tail overhang call for more caution on rough ground.

The significance of – left to right – approach angle, departure angle and ramp angle.

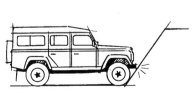  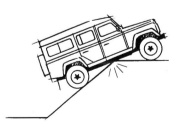

...continued

Land Rover Experience

Geometric limitations – continued

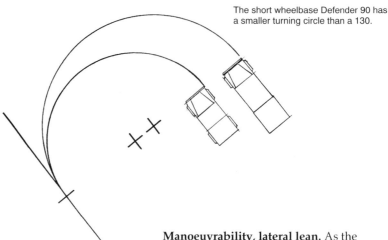

The short wheelbase Defender 90 has a smaller turning circle than a 130.

Manoeuvrability

A short wheelbase vehicle will be more agile than one with a long wheelbase.

Axle movement. We have already seen that articulation is the amount by which one axle can move – left wheel up, right wheel down or vice versa – in relation to the chassis and its fellow axle. Clearly it represents the degree to which your vehicle can keep its wheels on the ground on undulating 'twisty' terrain and thus retain traction under difficult conditions. All Land Rover products have very good articulation due to having coil springs and large wheel travel. But for a given amount of articulation – say a 40 cm lift under one front wheel before the other front wheel begins to lift – a shorter wheelbase actually represents a greater 'twisty ground' capability than a long wheelbase. So do not expect your Defender 130, although it has about the same axle articulation as a Defender 90 (assuming full wheel movement), to be able to traverse equally tortuous ground without lifting a wheel. See 'longitudinal articulation angle', Glossary, p 154 and tech data pages.

Axle articulation permits the ultimate 'twisty ground' performance; keeps wheels on ground and producing traction.

Manoeuvrability, lateral lean. As the diagram shows, the shorter the wheelbase the tighter the turning circle. The angle to which the vehicle can lean laterally without tipping is very similar on all models with standard bodywork . As covered in Section 4, 'Traversing slopes', p 54, this is a static figure and should not be relied on when driving. Local bumpiness and the effect of even minor steering corrections make a considerable difference and a limit of half the figures shown is recommended.

Land Rover products' long wheel travel gives exceptional articulation, ensuring optimum off-road performance.

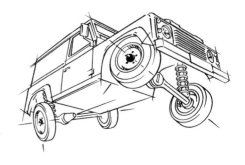

Land Rover Experience

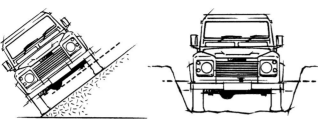

Land Rover do not quote exact lateral lean limits; exercise extreme caution at all times. See also p 54. Do not wade without fitting wading plugs – see p 68.

Wading depth. Maximum wading depth (see also Section 4, 'Wading', p 68) is quoted as 0.5 metre but for special circumstances using diesel engines and a raised air intake this can be increased.

Inspection first. When close to any of the above limitations a preliminary survey on foot is what is required, preferably with someone to marshal you through or round the obstacle. Whilst all Land Rover products are tough and capable off-road vehicles, it is pointless to risk underbody damage or getting stuck for the want of properly surveying the obstacle first. This is fully dealt with in the next spread.

If you are close to the limits, get out and take a closer look – see next spread.

Photos show uses of articulation (left) in crossing ditch – see p 46. Note gentle bow-wave when wading – see p 68. Side slopes always feel worse than they are – but don't press your luck!

LOOK BEFORE YOU LEAP

On-foot survey

Always make an on-foot inspection of difficult obstacles.

Inspect before you drive. It is invariably beneficial to do an on-foot survey of difficult obstacles before committing the vehicle. The aim of the survey is to pick the best route and ensure there are no previously unnoticed hazards such as rocks to foul the axles, deep ruts hidden in undergrowth or the lie of firm ground under snow. A reconnaissance also gives you the chance to test the firmness of visible ground – soft mud or the strength of the sand crust on a dune.

Use an external marshaller to direct you where clearances are tight.

Prod before you drive. An on-foot recce is especially important when fording streams and rivers where there is no established safe path. Nor will it be easy since you will have to establish not only the firmness of the river bed but also its evenness. Dropping into an underwater rock hole or suddenly descending to a depth that will drown the engine will require fundamental and major recovery procedures. Water deeper than about 35 cm demands that wading plugs be fitted to the clutch housing and cam-belt drive housing. (See 'Wading', p 68.)

Always worth it. An on-foot survey will delay you and is usually mucky or wet. It is, however, far preferable to damaging the Land Rover or finding you have a major recovery problem on your hands.

Marshalling

External guidance – marshalling. If you are not alone, an invaluable adjunct to negotiating difficult ground with small clearances is to have your passenger marshal you through from outside the vehicle. Only someone outside the vehicle can properly see all four wheels and where they are going – and see the exact clearances under the axle casings.

Overall view, take it steady. A marshaller should stand 5 to 15 metres ahead of the

On-foot inspection especially important in rivers where hazards are hidden.

On-foot pre-inspection establishes feasibility. Marshaller can see all four wheels, gives precision guidance and can avoid tyre damage on rocks.

vehicle – facing it – where all the wheels can easily be seen. Guidance by the marshaller should be given unambiguously and entirely by hand and arm signals rather than by voice. At the risk of stating the obvious, be sure there is just one marshaller who is in total charge and make a conscious effort to take things one step at a time. Situations in which marshalling is required frequently spawn two or three people all shouting half-heard directions at one time; the general tension often generates a feeling that something decisive and effective must be done, immediately...!

The calm and measured approach is to be preferred!

Marshaller in control. Obey the marshaller completely. Try not to take your eyes off him or her to make your own judgements on a situation you cannot assess as comprehensively as someone outside the vehicle. Stop if you are not happy but once moving, the marshaller is in control.

One marshaller only in control. Directions by signs, not voice.

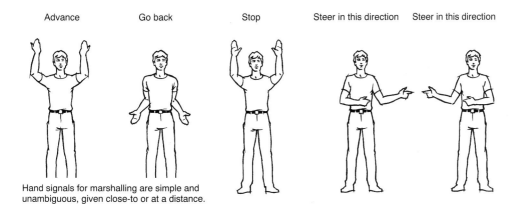

| Advance | Go back | Stop | Steer in this direction | Steer in this direction |

Hand signals for marshalling are simple and unambiguous, given close-to or at a distance.

SECTION 4

OPERATIONS – THE DETAILS

TOWING – ON-ROAD

From top is RTC9565 3500 kg limit ball – also with twin rear towing shackles, see p 89. Combination 3500 kg tow ball/jaw RTC8159, variable height. Four-bolt-fixing hitch cleared for 3500 kg on ball, 5000 kg on pin. Below is military 'NATO' type pintle.

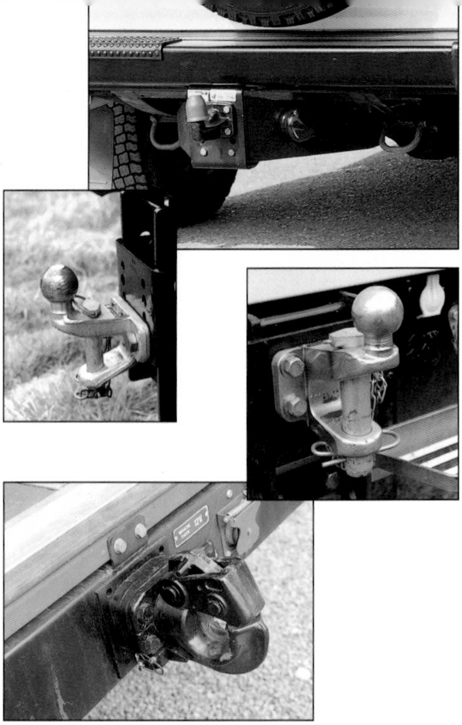

Setting-up the trailer

National regulations concern lighting and speed limits with trailers.

Regulated use and maxima. The Defender, Discovery and Range Rover are capable of towing trailers with gross on-road weights of up to 4000 kg and as such are subject to a range of international regulations for trailers regarding lighting, braking systems and speed limits. Buying a trailer from a reputable manufacturer will usually ensure that it complies with appropriate regulations. This section deals with the parameters involved and driving techniques. See p 102 for off-road towing.

Further national rules govern braking systems required at given gross trailer weights.

Braking and weight. Braking method and capacity are especially important. Design and regulatory limitations applicable to all Land Rover products are shown below. Above 3500 kg trailer gross weight coupled brakes are mandatory (photos p 41) but may be beneficial below this where required. Single or twin line air or vacuum brakes with various reservoirs may be fitted. Fitment of such systems requires specialist knowledge and standards of workmanship and should only be carried out by Special Vehicles department at Land Rover or their designated agents.

Two or four wheels, moments of inertia. The dynamics of trailers affect the towing vehicle – a long, heavy, trailer with a widely distributed load has a considerable moment of inertia; ie once any movement – lateral or vertical – has been initiated it will tend to continue and will be felt on the vehicle (see also diagrams pp 102/3). Try to concentrate the load low down and close to the axle. Close coupled four-wheel

Then there are manufacturer's clearances governing the weight you can tow with a given vehicle.

Maximum gross trailer weight (subject to local regulations)

Trailer/braking	On/off road	Defender with 2.5D kg	Defender with any other engine kg	Discovery kg	Range Rover kg
1. Unbraked trailer	On road Off road	750 500	750 500*	750 500†	750 750
2. Trailer with overrun brakes	On road Off road	3500 1000	3500 1000	3500** 1000†	3500 1000
3. 4-wheel trailer with coupled brakes (para above).	On road Off road	3500 1000	4000 1000	4000† 1000†	4000 1000

** 750 kg for 110 with self-levelled suspension. **Discovery Mpi 2750 kg †Not Discovery Mpi*

General towing considerations

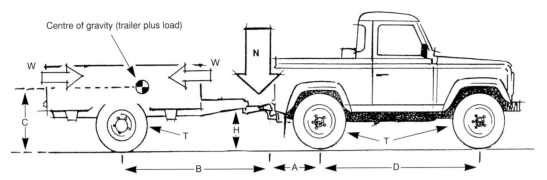

Centre of gravity (trailer plus load)

A/D – minimise (small A, big D) when considering a towing vehicle.
A/B – minimise (small A, big B) when considering a trailer.
C/B – C not to exceed 40% of B.
          C not to exceed 95% of trailer track (small C, wide track).
D/B – Small D, big B makes for easier reversing.
T – Tyre pressures – hard: GVW settings (p 112–114) unless off road (p 102).
H – Same for trailer and towing vehicle.
N – Trailer nose weight. More nose weight equals more towing stability – 7% of trailer
          gross weight a good starting point, BUT:
                1. Do not exceed limits of ball hitch or coupling head – usually 100–150 kg.
                2. Remove twice this amount from towing vehicle payload – ie if N = 75 kg,
                take 150 kg off listed max payload of vehicle when working out how much
                else you can carry in towing vehicle.
W – For a given nose weight, concentrate load close to trailer axle if possible to reduce
          moment of inertia.

Note: Height of centre of gravity C is drawn to scale here at maximum recommended
height above ground for this drawbar. Note how low that really is.

trailers exhibit broadly similar dynamics to two-wheel trailers but, for reasons of tyre loads are more suitable for high gross weights. A turntable trailer (also next page) is stable in its own right, has no 'tail wagging' effect and affects the towing vehicle in the fore and aft sense only.

General towing considerations. The diagram above encapsulates all the criteria relevant to optimum load and stability in a trailer and should be studied carefully in relation first to your particular requirements and then to the trailer/tug combination you have. Nose load is critically important to towing stability when setting up a given trailer.

Tow hitch, coupling head strength. The towing hitch and coupling head should be appropriate for the weight of the trailer. Remember that the widely used 50 mm ball hitch is limited to a 3500 kg trailer gross weight. Above this trailer weight use one of the hitches shown opposite.

Rear axle load. The download on the towing hitch is like having payload far aft of the centre of the vehicle load bed – check the diagram on p 123 and you will see that 250 kg carried on the tailgate actually increases the rear axle load by 341 kg. The same obviously applies to trailer nose load; see Note 2 under 'N' in diagram above.

Electrics, reversing. Lights, brake lights and direction indicators should be checked with the trailer and electrics connected. If your trailer has overrun brakes be sure you can inhibit them when reversing.

Trailer nose load is critical to stability.

Be sure too that you are within the strength limits of the tow hitch.

...continued

Towing on-road – continued

Driving with a trailer

Always check brakes. Although light, unbraked trailers will seem not to affect the vehicle very much it is wise to check overall braking action as soon as possible after starting off. Trailers with overrun brakes – especially if they have not been used for some time – can suffer from grabby, non-progressive brakes due to rusty brake drums and a test on a clear piece of road is essential before setting off with a newly loaded trailer. Whilst coupled brakes should be more progressive, a test is still wise since the trailer may not be proportionally braked and still exert some residual push on the towing vehicle during braking.

Beware full-lock. Instances have occurred where a full lock turn by the towing

As soon as you are moving, check braking response and behaviour.

Where vehicles are in continuous heavy-duty industrial use it is especially important that tow hitches and brakes systems chosen are appropriate to the maximum loads towed and that fleet use is properly monitored. Front-mounted hitch can be invaluable for precise manoeuvring and positioning.

vehicle with a short wide trailer brings the rear corner of the tow vehicle into contact with the front corner of the trailer – an indication that the tow bar is not long enough.

Reversing. Reversing with a trailer is a well known difficulty for drivers not used to it. In general, trailers which are long relative to the wheelbase of the towing vehicle (such as articulated trucks) are easier to reverse than those that are short. Those that are shorter than the wheelbase

Gross trailer weights above 3500 kgs and up to the maximum of 4000 kg demand a ring-hitch and coupled brakes – a special modification to the vehicle. Top and centre pictures (left) show electrically driven compressor unit and associated couplings for air brakes (as opposed to vacuum brakes) – a Land Rover Special Vehicles fit; lower shot shows heavyweight turn-table trailer which is stable but brings its own reversing problems.

of the vehicle are all but impossible to reverse any distance. As with all aspects of operating your Land Rover, do not be afraid to admit you have got it wrong. If a trailer is that short, it will also be light and uncoupling to manoeuvre it by hand will save the difficulty of trying to reverse it.

Manoeuvring; front hitch. Fitment and use of a front bumper towing hitch will be invaluable if you undertake a lot of towing and precision parking. Visibility is especially enhanced.

Excessive braking. Harsh braking when towing causes the trailer to increase down load on the towing vehicle hitch (hence need for centre of gravity constraints, diagram p 39). This produces a rotating moment about the rear axle and a resulting off-loading of the vehicle front wheels which can, in slippery conditions produce front wheel lock-up. This will not happen with ABS brakes and the risk can be reduced by use of cadence braking (p 28).

Towing off-road – see Section 6, p 102.

The knack of reversing is easier with a long trailer than a short one.

DRIVING ON TRACKS

Existing wheel tracks

Driving – smooth, calm. When a rough track is encountered your driving technique should aim to have the vehicle flow smoothly over it rather than jolt and jar. All current Land Rover products are coil sprung front and rear with progressive dampers so this will be easier basically to achieve than on most other makes of off-road vehicle. The application of the mechanical sympathy mentioned on p 26 will do much to foster an appropriately smooth driving technique for these conditions. Taking a calm and unhurried approach will also help.

Aim to flow smoothly over rough terrain – don't let the vehicle jolt and jar.

High gears, low range. As mentioned before (Section 2 – 'Low range – when and how', p 20) the high gears in the low range are often very useful on rough tracks. Such tracks usually have short, difficult sections for which the steady control of the low range will be required without constant use of the brake and clutch pedals. Thus taking a track at a steady pace in, say, 5th gear low ratio will give the driver the opportunity to change right down to 2nd or even 1st where the ultimate low speed control and torque is available. (High range, of course, is sometimes quite adequate; to get a clear picture of the overlap between high and low range gears, see Section 6 – 'High/low range overlap', p 94.)

High gears in the low box very useful for rough tracks.

Railway line effect. Driving along a deeply rutted track where the ruts are cut into slippery ground can be like driving along railway lines; turning the steering wheel left or right does not have any effect since the tyres will not grip on the steep slippery sides of the ruts. The danger of this situation is that you can be driving along

Let self-centring castor-action periodically align your wheels in deep ruts.

Deep ruts with slippery sides can mask normal steering feedback. You can be unaware your wheels are not pointing straight ahead and when grip is available, vehicle suddenly veers. See also Glossary, 'Steering feel', p 157.

with some steering lock applied (which the vehicle is not responding to) and not know it. When the vehicle reaches level ground or a patch where traction permits it to respond to the steering lock applied, the vehicle will suddenly veer off the track with possibly dangerous consequences.

Wheels straight ahead? Since this condition is not met every day it is doubly important to have the possibility in the back of your mind that the prevailing conditions may be of this type when you are in ruts. The way to preclude the occurrence is to monitor the self-centring of the steering; periodically reduce your grip

Typical rough tracks have moderately fast sections (above) for which 5th low ratio may be ideal. Low ratio enables you to change down to a cautious 2nd for the really rough bits (left).

on the steering wheel by keeping just a frictional grip with the palms of your hands, letting it regain, through castor action (see p 148), the straight ahead position. Also a visual check from the driver's window will establish which way the wheels are pointing. When using the window in this way beware of branches of shrubs or trees flicking in your face.

Existing wheel tracks – traction. If there are already wheel tracks along the unsurfaced road you are travelling, this can affect the traction of your vehicle – for better or for worse. On wet or muddy tracks or in snow it is best to follow in the tracks of a previous vehicle since, in general terms, that vehicle will probably have cut through to the drier ground beneath and this will offer your vehicle more traction. See also Sections – 'Climbing steep slopes' (p 48) and 'Soft ground', p 56.

Desert and bush. On sandy tracks in desert or bush or on routes over desert plains avoid the tracks of previous vehicles since they will have broken the thin crust that normally forms on wind blown sand. Beneath this crust is soft sand offering less flotation; often this is badly churned which will make flotation and traction even worse. See 'Soft sand', p 60.

Beware driving with non-gripping steering lock on.

Drive in previous wheel-tracks in mud and snow, but not in soft sand.

...continued

Driving on tracks – continued

Fast relatively smooth tracks are one of the delights of 'off-road' driving but you should always be on your guard against sudden deterioration and the reduced braking the loose surface causes. Muddy tracks call for a delicate right foot.

Deep ruts, gullies

Be on the lookout for ruts that have become gullies. They will run you out of under-axle clearance.

Under-axle clearance. Rough tracks will sometimes deteriorate into deep V-shaped gullies due to water erosion or extra deep ruts caused by the passage of trucks with big wheels. Keeping in such ruts will lead to grounding the chassis or axle case of your Land Rover vehicle and anticipation is needed to take appropriate action before getting into difficulties. As the diagram shows, you should aim to get out of the ruts early so as to straddle the gully. Great care will be necessary to avoid steering up

one or other of the gully walls which could lead to the vehicle being trapped with its side against the gully.

Steering feel. As indicated on p 42, because of the depth or slipperiness of the rut or gully, you may well lose the natural feel of the steering and find it hard to know exactly which way your wheels are pointing. For this reason and to ensure front and back wheels are surveyed all the time when driving over gullies, use a

Rain or flood erosion can cause deep ruts to become gullies and there is the danger of the vehicle slipping down one side. Careful guidance by a marshaller who can see all wheels is the only way to negotiate this kind of obstacle.

Do not stay in badly eroded ruts (1). Get out of ruts and (2) straddle the gully. Vehicle must be carefully guided in gully to sit evenly across it. If necessary, cut steps with a shovel to give tyres a positive footing.

1.

2.

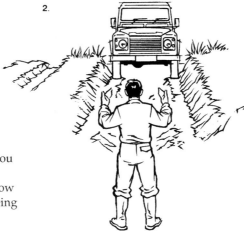

You will lose steering feel driving gully sides. Get guidance and/or look out of the window.

marshaller ahead of the vehicle giving you precise directions. If you do not have a marshaller then lower the driver's window and observe the front wheel yourself, being careful, as already mentioned, of tree or bush branches flicking in your face.

RIDGES AND DITCHES

Diagonal suspension

Ridge – a mirror-image ditch. Ridges and ditches can be encountered both on tracks and across open country. Though one is a mirror image of the other, ridges and ditches can introduce the same problems for the vehicle – grounding the chassis or hanging diagonally-opposite wheels in the air and losing traction by reaching the limits of articulation. The method of crossing these obstacles will require judgement according to their size since the recommended method of crossing a small ridge will lead to trouble if it is applied to a big (or abrupt) one.

Diagonal wheel-spin is the main hazard. Know your vehicle's articulation limits.

Size determines technique

Potential hazards. The diagram shows the potential hazards and the best general advice is to take ridges and ditches diagonally with as much momentum as you judge to be prudent. If that seems like the ultimate escape clause, consider these obstacles in three sizes:

Methods of crossing ridges and ditches vary according to the size of the obstacle.

1. Small ridges and ditches. These may be taken at right angles within the limits dictated by vehicle underbelly clearance and rear overhang (departure angle). However this does mean that the respective front and rear axles will hit the obstacle square-on and probably impart an undesirable jolt. By taking the obstacles diagonally the vehicle will flow over the obstacle with a rolling motion but without any shock loading. Indeed if, when driving quickly over a plain you encounter a shallow ditch which you had not seen

Diagonal approach is always best – but beware severe ridges and ditches.

'Landscaping' – digging under the hung-up wheels – will lower the vehicle so that all four wheels are in contact with the ground and traction is regained.

earlier, alter direction immediately to take it diagonally.

2. Medium sized ridges and ditches. These may be classified as those that will give problems of underbelly or departure angle clearance and therefore cannot be taken at right angles. With these ones you thus have no option but to take them diagonally. The technique outlined above should be used.

3. Tall ridges and deep ditches. On-foot inspection and the assistance of a marshaller will almost certainly be necessary. These are obstacles that

Land Rover Experience

Photographs show on-the-limits articulation as vehicles cross ridges and ditches. 'Hanging' wheels have little load in this situation so could spin if provoked. Aim for optimum balance of momentum and throttle.

definitely cannot be taken at right angles and also, if taken slowly diagonally, will result in diagonally-opposite wheels lifting to allow wheel spin and loss of traction. In these cases you have two options:

a. *Provided the going is smooth enough* take the obstacle diagonally but fast enough for momentum to carry the vehicle past the momentary lifting of corner wheels.

b. *Provided it is permitted*, 'landscape' the ground with a shovel to remove the top of the ridge or edge of the ditch that will cause grounding of the chassis or tail end

or suspension of the wheels and then proceed as at 1 above.

Learning gently. As with so many skills it takes longer to write and read this advice than to apply it. You will quickly learn to judge which situation you are in. So long as you do not jolt the vehicle badly or ground the chassis it does not matter if you do not get this right first time – at least on small and medium obstacles. As ever, do not be afraid to take it gently at first or admit you got it wrong; back off and try again – no damage has been done. (See also 'Self recovery', p 78.)

Judgement required: speed and diagonal approach can help. Digging under hung-up wheels may be needed.

CLIMBING STEEP SLOPES
Grip, gradient, momentum

Grip and gradient. The twin problems with steep slopes – gradient and grip – usually reduce themselves to one in most cases with a Land Rover since all Land Rover products have the power and appropriate gearing to climb a continuous slope of nearly 1-in-1 or 45° if the grip is there. Grip is far more likely to be the limiting factor and we have seen in Section 3 – 'Gentle right foot' (p 28) how use of the right gear (not necessarily the lowest one) allied to a sensitive right foot can eliminate the wheel-spin that can result from insufficient grip. Climbing steep slopes is the classic application of sensing grip and being gentle with the throttle – and, see below, admitting defeat early in cases of wheel spin. Don't floor the throttle when you get wheel-spin in the vain hope of getting up the slope; the vehicle could slide sideways off course and may tip – see diagram, right.

Grip invariably the limiting factor on steep slopes. The right gear (usually 2nd or 3rd low) and a sensitive throttle foot is the answer.

Go straight at the slope. Whilst a walker would take diagonal tacks up a steep hill to reduce the gradient, you should take the fall line direct in a vehicle, ie take the slope at right angles, head-on. This is to ensure the vehicle is laterally level – your walker can stand up straight when traversing a steep hill; a vehicle leans over (see 'Traversing slopes' – p 54) and is in danger of tipping down the slope in extreme cases.

Momentum, traction, throttle control. Commonsense steep slopes need no more than commonsense tactics: if it is reasonably smooth and not excessively steep take a bit of a run at it in the right gear and do not over-torque the wheels to provoke wheel spin. Select the right gear before the slope and stay in it; only an automatic will do a smooth enough change if one is needed. But on really difficult slopes, as ever, an on-foot survey will help. Such slopes are unlikely to be smooth and

Keep at right angles to the slope – going up or when reversing back down – see next spread.

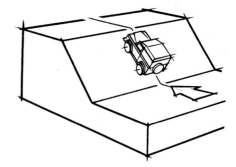

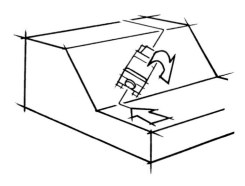

Going up a slope at right angles to the lip of the ridge is safe; a diagonal approach can provoke a roll-over down the slope. The risk is made worse by any wheel-spin.

tramping out the chosen route to locate any local bumps, tree stumps or rabbit holes that might cause a wheel to lift will be useful.

Extra grip – from the steering wheel. If the track is rutted – and this can apply on level ground too – limiting grip can be enhanced by moving the steering wheel from side to side (10 o'clock to 2 o'clock) and cause the tyre sidewalls to contribute grip.

Higher gear – with lift-off. Unless you are tackling an unusual and exceptional climb

Classic example (above) of a 2nd gear low box slope needing a bit of momentum at the bottom and a readiness to lift off the throttle towards the top. One of the rare 1st gear low box slopes where grip permits full use of gradability (left).

such as 40° on rough dry concrete, 1st gear low box will be too low and will provoke wheel-spin. Most 'normal severe' climbs will be best tackled in 2nd gear low box, or, if there is any amount of run-up available, 3rd. Use the most run-up momentum you can, having established the ground is smooth enough to permit it, since the more you can utilise this, the less will be the demand for grip from the ground actually on the slope. As you near the top of the slope your momentum may be running out and the vehicle will become more reliant on grip and traction. This is the point (quite near to the top) where the wheels are most likely to start slipping or spinning – and it is thus, paradoxically, the point where you may find that lifting off the throttle helps put that final bit of power on the ground without spinning the wheels.

Automatic applications. The equivalent of lift-off to de-stress the ground where traction is marginal will occur on an auto transmission vehicle if 3rd is selected before a steep climb. The gearbox will change to 3rd as the throttle is lifted and reduce the risk of wheel-spin.

Be prepared to lift off near the top to preclude wheel-spin.

...continued

Land Rover Experience

Climbing steep slopes – continued

Failed climb, recovery

First-time scare. If you are losing grip don't boot the throttle and accentuate the wheel-spin; de-clutch and apply the footbrake. Your first failed steep climb – bonnet pointing at the sky, brake leg trembling, maybe a dead engine and a plan view of the world in your rear view mirror – can be mildly scaring; it can sometimes also be mechanically traumatic for the vehicle if a driver tries to bluff it out or attempt impossibly quick sequences of control selections during the 'recovery' descent.

Slowing the adrenalin. Observing – and practising – the following procedures makes a failed climb so matter-of fact and relaxed that anxiety as to whether you will make it up the slope first time disappears and both driver and vehicle have a far easier time. Knowing that failing and trying again is no real problem means you do not cane the vehicle unnecessarily hard on the first white-knuckle attempt. Climbs can fail with or without a dead engine:

1. Forward motion ceases, engine stalled – gradient problem.

2. Forward motion ceases, engine running, wheels spinning – grip problem.

Using the following procedure you will come back down the hill with both hands on the steering wheel (important, that), feet off the pedals – ie not on clutch, or footbrake but covering the throttle – with engine braking controlling your speed of descent and no frantic use of gear lever or handbrake. (Procedure for manual transmission shown; *Auto* procedure is shown in brackets)

Just as you would always go up a slope at right angles to the maximum gradient, do the same coming back down.

Remember that in reverse, steering castor action is also reversed. Grip the wheel firmly to prevent 'runaway'.

Engage reverse with the engine dead. Foot off clutch, touch the starter.

Failed climb, stalled engine. If you have failed the climb and stalled the engine in the process (see also diagram sequence opposite):

1. Hold the vehicle on the footbrake, clutch position immaterial. (*Auto:* go to step 5.)

2. Engage reverse gear low box and remove left foot from clutch.

3. With both hands on the steering wheel, slowly lessen the pressure on the footbrake until your foot is off it. The vehicle is now held by the engine.

4. The vehicle may begin to move backwards on its own and in so doing 'bump'-start the engine. In which case let it continue, under full control of engine braking, keeping both hands firmly on the steering wheel. Remember that in reverse, steering castor action is also reversed and there is a tendency for the steering wheel to 'run-away' to full lock if you do not hold it firmly.

5. If the engine has not started under gravity, take one hand off the wheel to operate the starter motor briefly – with the vehicle still in reverse gear and clutch fully engaged. This will invariably kick the engine into life and you are, as in 4. above, slowly descending back down the slope in full control, in gear, clutch fully engaged, left foot on the floor, both hands on steering wheel, right foot hovering over throttle. (*Auto:* foot still on brake, select '**N**' or '**P**', start engine, engage '**R**', both hands on wheel, slowly release footbrake.)

6. Just as you would *climb* the slope at right angles to the gradient, make sure you go straight back down the slope – still at right angles to the gradient. When you reach less steep ground, use the controls in the normal way.

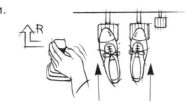

1.

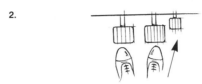

2.

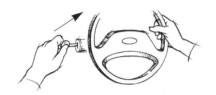

3.

Recovery sequence, stalled engine – list, facing page. 1. Clutch, footbrake, into reverse. 2. Feet off all pedals – but throttle foot ready. 3. Touch the starter briefly; both hands on steering wheel. Preferably reverse back on mirrors.

Failed climb, engine running. If you have failed the climb through loss of grip and wheel-spin:

1. Hold the vehicle on the footbrake, clutch pedal depressed, engine idling. (*Auto:* allow engine revs to die, engage '**R**' low box, gently release brake, jump to step 4.)

2. Engage reverse gear low box.

3. With both hands on the steering wheel and leading with the clutch, release the clutch and footbrake. The vehicle (engine still idling) will start back down the slope fully controlled by engine braking. As above, at this stage your feet can be off all three pedals – ie you are in reverse, clutch fully engaged and engine idling.

4. Keeping both hands on the steering wheel, as above, to resist any steering 'run-away', and go straight back down the slope to less steep ground.

5. Note. The admit-defeat-early credo is very important in a traction failure on a hill – ie with spinning wheels. If you do not quit the moment it is clear you are not going to make it, it is very likely the vehicle, wheels spinning on a slippery surface, will slew sideways-on to the slope and there is a risk of it capsizing down the hill. Even if it does not do this, the wheels – usually one front wheel with its diagonally opposite back wheel – will scoop depressions in the ground to make your next attempt more difficult.

Aim after a failed climb is to come straight back down the slope, both hands on the wheel, feet off pedals.

The nub of a safe failed-climb descent – feet off all the pedals (but throttle-ready) and the vehicle going back down – STRAIGHT and under engine braking. Nothing to fear getting it wrong even on slopes like this (below).

DESCENDING STEEP SLOPES

Gear to use

Remove the drama. Land Rover vehicles' extraordinary agility may make your first really steep descent an intimidating experience. A 45° down-slope itself is unusual enough but to this angle you add the fact that you are looking even further downward over the bonnet; the result can seem vertical, especially when you are hanging forward in your seat harness. But this is an experience that you will very quickly get used to – usually after just one steep descent. As with climbs, the aim is to take the drama out of the situation and utilise the vehicle's facility for keeping you in control.

The view over the bonnet comes only when you are committed to the slope; so recce on foot first. The ideal descent is with both feet on the floor and the engine doing the braking.

Stop 2m from the edge (engine off, 1st gear, handbrake) and inspect on foot. Plan to use engine braking.

Get out and look. A 45° slope is extreme but there are many lesser slopes that can still seem very steep and, as with the climb, an on-foot inspection is advisable to ensure that your planned route is safe. This is doubly important since when you come to the edge of a steep descent you can sometimes see nothing over the bonnet except the other side of the dip; only when you are actually pointing down the slope can you see the ground immediately in front of you. (For this reason, among others, stop the vehicle for the on-foot inspection at least two metres before the edge of the slope – engine off, in gear, handbrake on. This will give you time, when you do start the descent, to get the vehicle fully in gear and with your foot off the clutch for the descent.)

Use 1st gear, low range, foot off the throttle to brake you down 99% of steep slopes – see p 100 for the other 1%.

Gear – rule of thumb, 1st gear low range. Using 1st gear low range will in nearly every case result in a perfectly controlled, feet-off-all-pedals descent. Actual retardation will be dependent upon

Retardation will will be greater with diesels and manual transmissions.

whether you have a diesel or petrol engine, whether or not it has a manual transmission and the condition of the slope but the rule is a good one and a safe one.

The rationale. Your aim is to obtain maximum retardation without resorting to the brakes which despite the sensitivity and feel of the disc brakes on Land Rover vehicles, can result in wheel locking and sliding. As always your aim is to preclude any possibility of discontinuity of rolling contact (see Section 3 – 'Gentle right foot', p 28) – ie no wheel-spinning or, more likely in this case, sliding.

Ready for throttle. If the ground is too slippery to provide the grip for the retardation of the throttle-off engine and you begin to slide, be ready to use the accelerator to help the wheels 'catch up'

with the vehicle and eliminate any wheel slide.

Ready for exceptions. There may be occasions – typically long descents of loose ground or extremely slippery clay, steep initially – where low ratio 2nd gear will be better in order to preclude an initial sliding-wheel glissade. One or two exceptions are covered on p 100-101. Some descents – see photo p 101 – will actually demand 3rd low range and considerable throttle to prevent nosing-in on a soft surface. As before, it is best to select the gear for the whole obstacle and stay in it.

Brakes

Brakes? Never... An easy generalisation - and for good reasons – is to counsel against ever using brakes on a steep slippery descent. Braking on wet, muddy or loose-surface slopes – even with the excellent sensitivity of the Land Rover's discs – can easily cause one or more wheels to lock and the loss of directional control in the resulting slide could be dangerous. The use of engine braking down steep slopes makes, in general, for a very safe, controlled way of keeping the vehicle from gaining speed and there is no danger of overheating the brakes. Often you are able to take both feet off the pedals and rest them flat on the floor while the vehicle trundles gently down the slope with the engine idling.

But... But there are times when engine braking is not the infallible solution and the sensitive use of brakes or, preferably, cadence braking can help (See Section 6 – 'Engine braking', p 100.)

Rule of thumb – 1st low and do not use the brakes. But... see p 100. Accelerate if necessary.

TRAVERSING SLOPES

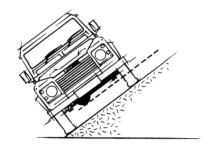

A *static rig-test* tip angle is around 40° but the dynamics of real driving make this dangerous to approach. Escape manoeuvre (below) applies if you feel you are getting close to tipping.

Assessing the ground

Side slopes are different. From the last two sections – 'Climbing steep slopes' and 'Descending steep slopes' – the doctrine of always taking such obstacles at right angles to the slopes implies that traversing a slope is dangerous. And so it can be when the angle of gradient is severe. There will be times, however, when, on less severe slopes, you do need to traverse the slope laterally. Like your first steep climb and descent, your first traverse will be unnerving. Unlike climbs and descents, however, you will not quickly get used to it. And that is a good thing since the consequences of getting it wrong on a traverse are a great deal more serious than getting it wrong on a climb or descent.

Side-slopes don't feel right. Trust your unease and treat them with great caution.

Trust your instincts. There appears to be a built-in safety feature of human perception that makes a traverse feel a lot more dangerous than it is. Your vehicle will actually tilt to quite high angles on perfectly smooth ground without rolling over but to the driver, a traverse along a slope even one third of the maximum permissible will feel alarming. Follow your instinct and do not traverse slopes that feel

As ever, inspect on foot looking for bumps or hollows that can affect vehicle's lateral stance.

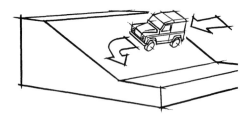

dangerous. As ever, carry out an on-foot reconnaissance first:

1. Slippery surface. Assess the surface to be sure it is not so slippery that the vehicle will slide sideways down the slope.

2. Bumps and dips. Look out for dips that the down-hill wheels may encounter and bumps that the up-hill wheels may roll over – rabbit holes and sawn-off tree stumps in particular. Both will increase the tilt of the vehicle and increase the risk of it

The on-foot inspection is especially important. Look for bumps or dips that affect lateral lean. Every inch of ground irregularity makes approximately 1° difference to lateral lean – a 4" bump equals 4°. Digging away the hillside ahead of the up-slope wheels can lower the actual tilt angle.

tipping over.

3. Secure load. Any load in the back of your vehicle should be secure and as low as possible. Be particularly wary of roof-rack loads. Passengers should sit on the up-hill side – or dismount.

4. Marshalling. If there are any doubts about the effect of the terrain or if there are obstacles to avoid, then use a marshaller to see you forward and make sure he or she keeps an eye on all four wheels.

Escape manoeuvre

Be ready. Steer down the hill if the vehicle slips or seems too close to the maximum tip angle. As with normal steep descents, the nearer you can get the vehicle pointing directly down the slope the less the danger of lateral tipping. If you feel the machine getting laterally unstable turn down the hill quickly and give a little burst of throttle. The centrifugal force of the quick turn, further enhanced by the blip of throttle, will help keep the vehicle upright.

'Escape' by steering down the hill, with a touch of throttle.

SOFT GROUND

Grassy lanes are classic examples of a combination of low vertical and low horizontal ground strength – a mixture of the soft and slippery. If a vehicle is used continuously on unstable ground, snow-chains can be a useful traction aid.

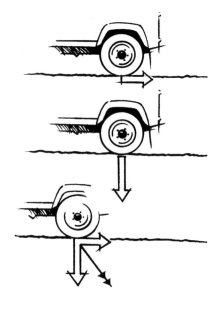

A 4x4 under power generates, on the ground, horizontal thrust (top) and vertical thrust (centre) to produce a resultant diagonal (bottom). Decreasing tyre pressure – weight per unit area – and exercising care with throttle and brakes reduces both components of ground stress. See also diagram p 12.

Ground stress – horizontal, vertical

Soft ground is weak laterally as well as vertically – so it's that gentle right foot again.

Reading the ground. Soft ground is weak ground – vertically and laterally as well. The vertical context is well known – the tendency for a vehicle to sink in it – and the lateral connotations mean it will not take much thrust (or braking) from wheels without degenerating into slippery wheel-spin (or slide); the gentle right foot on brakes and throttle (Section 3, p 28) comes into its own. Soft ground is rarely uniformly soft – a fairly obvious statement but one to highlight the need for reading the surface and adjusting your throttle foot accordingly; getting the traction where you can, backing off where you can afford to do so in order not to lose the traction you do have.

Lock the centre diff, read the ground, judge what it will take without spinning the wheels.

Horizontal load – throttle and brakes. The most immediate control you have when encountering soft ground is from within the vehicle. You should be in four wheel drive – which you are in all current Land Rover products – and the centre differential should be locked so as to preclude the possibility of one axle spinning any faster than the other. No hard and fast rule can be

Examples of ground that is vertically weak (soft, left), horizontally weak (slippery, below left) and close to the limit on both – below.

laid down as to the 'best' action then to take. Some situations will demand you accelerate on the good going to take you through the soft patch using momentum, others will demand you slow down to take it gently because it is uneven or of extended length. The only invariable rule is to heighten your awareness of the risk of wheel-spin and to take appropriate action with the controls. Choose the highest gear you judge will get you through without either wheel-spin or over-stressing the engine – this will often be 2nd or 3rd low range. As for brakes, remember they stress the ground in the same way as driving torque at the wheels and insensitivity will result in sliding or, in sand, breaking the crust.

Low range 2nd or 3rd will usually be the gears for soft ground.

...continued

Land Rover Experience

Soft ground – continued

Tyre pressures

Vertical load – per square inch. Vertical load per unit area – the tyre pressures, rather than total vertical load – is most often what you will have easiest control of. Tyre pressures may not initially be thought to make much difference since the total weight of the vehicle will usually remain the same and sitting on the same four tyres. But bear in mind that 'emergency flotation' pressures can be two thirds of road pressures or less. This means that the tyre footprint increases in size (see diagrams pp 12 and 113) and the weight of the vehicle is spread over a correspondingly larger area so that – as in recognising the benefits of 4x4 which spreads the thrust over four instead of two wheels – you are asking less of the ground that is already having difficulty in supporting the vehicle's weight.

Reduced tyre pressures – when and how much. Reduce pressures only when needed – then re-inflate (see 'Rock, stones, corrugations', p 64). The golden rule is not to run with low tyre pressures without reducing your speed; if you do not, serious overheating of the tyre could occur which, in extreme cases, could lead to tyre damage. Additionally, with inappropriately low tyre pressures the steering and handling of the vehicle will be adversely affected. Tyre pressures for particular conditions will vary according to the vehicle, the axle load and the manufacturer of the tyres. Typical axle loads and off-road tyre pressures for Land Rover vehicles are given in Section 7, 'Tyres', pp 111-114. Rule-of-thumb guidance figures are shown below:

1. Tracks and poor roads – 80% of road pressures, maximum speed 65 kph (40 mph).

2. Emergency flotation pressures – about 60% of road pressures, maximum speed 20 kph (12 mph).

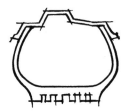

Radial tyres (above and Glossary p 155), as well as many other advantages over cross-ply tyres (below and Glossary p 149) have thinner sidewalls which more easily accept the flexing inevitable with reduced pressures. But see also p 65 re cross-ply advantages.

Length of ground contact patch increases with lowered tyre pressures – see diagrams pp 12 and 113 – to improve flotation. Sidewall flexing also increases – the reason why re-inflation is important when higher speeds are resumed. Picture shows radial tyre reduced to 1.1 bar (16 psi); beware sidewall damage – see p 64.

Regular operation on and off tracks such as this (right) with a never-exceed speed of 40 mph would benefit from reduced tyre pressures. Emergency flotation pressures would be appropriate in difficult conditions (below) at 20 kph (12 mph) max. Tyres must be re-inflated for normal operation; there is also a legal requirement that tyres used on public roads must be properly inflated.

Vertical load – reducing the total. It is commonsense that reducing the overall load will give the vehicle a better chance in soft going. Quantitatively, as indicated in Section 7, 'Tyres', p 108, this will reduce axle load, particularly at the rear, and enable quite marked reduction in tyre pressure to be used. In practical terms few users will be able to dispose of payload to suit the going but the principle is worth remembering for the extreme case of a bogged vehicle - see 'Self-Recovery', p 78.

Previous wheel tracks. As already mentioned ('Driving on tracks', p 42), if the soft ground is wet or muddy, it will usually pay to follow the wheel tracks of a previous vehicle since that vehicle will have cut through to firmer ground and you will be able to take advantage of that. If the soft ground is sandy see next section.

Tyres for soft ground. There are specialist tyres optimised for different types of terrain; see Section 7 , 'Tyres', p 109.

Choice of tyres is important for frequent soft-ground operation – see p 109.

Land Rover Experience

SOFT SAND

Initial rules

There are many types and conditions of sand – all with characteristic bearing strengths.

Different types. Wet sand, damp sand and a dozen types and conditions of dry sand each lead to different expectations of vertical and horizontal strength (flotation and surface shear strength) as well as behaving differently as far as compaction strength is concerned. Each thus demands different driving techniques. Avoiding wheel-spin, already a golden rule of off-road driving, is nowhere more important than in sand. All, where there is doubt, demand on-foot inspection and 'stamping out' to ascertain firmness and, when close to the limits, the vehicle will have a far better chance if tyre pressures are reduced – see diagrams pp 12 and 113 and tyre pressure/speed limit tables pp 112-114.

When a track starts getting difficult try high box diff lock or low box 4th or 5th with diff lock.

Initial rule-of-thumb. Initial guide rules are therefore in order if you are to get through the sand rather than trying to learn all the different varieties of problem at once.

1. Dry sand. If you are running out of traction or flotation, keep off previously churned or broken sand. Make your own new tracks.

2. Damp sand. Follow previous tracks which will have compacted the sand and made it firmer.

If the going has been churned up, break out of the track onto unbroken sand. It will be stronger.

3. Wet sand. Keep off altogether. It can contain areas of 'floating' sand, or quicksand – bottomless with virtually no vertical strength.

4. Sebkha (salt flat). Very dangerous – unpredictably soft and bottomless. If a well-used track goes over a sebkha it will have compacted the surface (seemingly from beneath) into a smooth, relatively strong route. Do not stray off the hardened track by even a tyre's width.

Innocuous-looking sebkha (above) can be extremely treacherous. Tracks (far right) can be difficult when previously traversed by large trucks; there is then a case for getting onto untrodden sand – rarely quite as firm as this example (right).

Sand types

Dry sand. Being an aggregate of small grains and large grains, nature's windblown sand, helped by night dews and diurnal heating and contracting, forms a surface crust which has more strength than the sand beneath; it is stronger in the cool of the morning than in the heat of the day. Use these characteristics to your advantage and be very careful not to break through into the soft sand beneath; think of the analogy of driving on a pie crust.

1. Sandy tracks. Sandy tracks, by reason of the previous passage of vehicles, have no pie crust. Difficulty is likely where there has been a lot of previous truck traffic. Three things will happen here – the ruts will get deeper, the depth of churned sand will increase and the width between the ruts will increase. This is simply a function of the size of the previous vehicles – their

Previously unbroken sand, particularly, has a 'pie crust' that can be surprisingly strong. But be careful with throttle and brakes.

wheel diameter and the width of their axles. As ever, be ready to admit defeat early – before getting into real trouble – and steer out of the track onto virgin ground if you can. The higher gears – 3rd, 4th and 5th – in the low box (centre diff locked) will probably be best for tracks of this kind. The advantage of *being* in low box is that it will enable you to accelerate through suddenly worsening conditions without the risk of being unable to restart, having stopped to change from high to low box. For this reason do not stop except on firm going – or if you do have to stop be gentle with the brakes. As the going gets heavier and more demanding you will find you have to be firm with the throttle and use a lot of the torque at your disposal; this is different from the technique used on virgin sand.

2. Virgin sand. Some desert sand is remarkably firm and strong. But if you are close to the limits of flotation when on virgin, unbroken sand in the open desert (or once out of the ruts on the track) you have to be more delicate with the throttle in order not to break the crust of clean sand supporting you. The same goes for the brakes and steering. On some dune surfaces there is a good case for letting the vehicle come to a rolling stop without brakes at all. Similarly, when stopping your vehicle on sand remember that re-starting when facing up a slope is almost impossible and you should therefore stop on level ground, or, if possible, with the vehicle facing downhill.

...continued

Land Rover Experience

Soft sand – continued

Sand types , dry sand – contd

Dune formations will have firm areas dependent on position relative to crest and valley.

3. Sand dunes. Small, closely packed dunes (up to around four metres high, and especially if randomly oriented) are better driven round rather than attempting to drive over them. When dunes are that small the sand is invariably loose and weak. Any dunes larger than 4–5 metres are usually sufficiently spaced out to permit driving between them and taking advantage of the firm areas. The variation of flotation over a dune structure is soon learned – the hard way. Whilst no two dune chains are the same, the diagram shows the general principles of where to expect the firm bits. Avoid the sand-falls completely. No vehicle will ever get up one but most are so soft that the vehicle will sink and lose steering-way even trying to descend one – but see photo p 101. Also in this context, see Glossary 'Caster angle', p 148 and 'Steering feel', p 157.

All sand has increased bearing strength if cold, dewy or rained-on.

Salt flat is inherently dangerous. Except on established tracks, keep off.

In general, going is firmer where the up-wind side of the dunes meet the valley floor.

Damp sand. Sand that is damp – such as it might be after a rain shower or even morning dew – just makes driving easier. The water binds it together, strengthens it, gives more flotation and on tracks actually makes it compact to yield considerably more strength than the dry, churned-up sand had before the rain.

Wet sand. It becomes a matter of judgement and definition to say when damp sand gets to be wet sand. Beach sand will frequently behave as dry, cut-up, churned sand where it is dry and become considerably firmer where it is washed by the tide – though this is not an invariable rule. The warning sounded earlier refers to really wet sand of the kind encountered where a river or stream meets the sea and where a kind of 'floating' sand is encountered. This is akin to a quicksand where motion by the person or vehicle on it just causes further sinkage.

Sebkha (salt flat). Sometimes also marked on maps as 'chott', a sebkha forms where lakes used to be and consists of a crust of dried salt-mud covering soft, bottomless salt-mud underneath. The crust is of variable and unpredictable strength but appears to have the curious characteristic of consolidating from underneath when progressively heavier vehicles run over it. Thus a track over a sebkha usually consists of wheel marks indented probably no more than a few centimetres into the surface – implying that the surrounding ground is firm. As the stern warning above indicates, however, this is not the case and straying off the track even a tyre width or a metre can result in disastrous sinkage. A vehicle stuck in sebkha will quickly sink to the chassis and sometimes go on sinking. It is usually impossible to effect self-recovery and even assisting vehicles should have very long tow ropes or winches in order that they too do not sink.

The classic desert tyre of all time, the Michelin XS – worn example at reduced pressure shown left – with a tread optimised to get the most traction out of all types of sand. Diagrams pp12, 113 show increase in footprint area of XS deflated to emergency soft. Certain parts of dunes can be surprisingly firm but (above left) even with the best tyres, the limits can be found.

Sand tyres. As already indicated (and covered more fully in Section 7, 'Tyres', p 108), each kind of terrain demands its own specialist tyre. This is particularly important in the case of sand. Even here the carefully named 'desert' tyre has to accommodate the different requirements of travel on rock and sand. In general, however, the greatest design conflict would be between a mud tyre and a sand tyre – the one requiring a bold angular tread and the sand tyre needing a far gentler, more subtle tread design. And whilst the sidewall of a desert tyre must be strong to resist rock damage it must also be flexible to accommodate the greatly reduced tyre pressures used in the worst sand conditions. If contemplating desert operations your vehicle's performance will be considerably enhanced if desert tyres are fitted. Section 7 shows tyre types, axle loads and tyre pressures for typical conditions. See also 'Sand tyres', p 156.

Getting stuck, recovery. Self-recovery and assisted recovery is covered later in this section (p 78 and p 82). Inevitably, sand is a little different. Just as inevitably, the recovery methods are commonsense honed with pragmatism and experience.

Fitting specialist desert tyres is particularly important in achieving optimum performance in sand.

ROCKS, STONES, CORRUGATIONS

Regular operation in rocky conditions demands extra awareness of under-axle clearance and of tyre sidewall vulnerability.

Risks – chassis, tyres

Under-axle and under body clearances dictate 20–30 cm rocks as about the maximum size to drive over.

Rocks – 30 cm high. The sections dealing with use of the low transfer box and the methods of driving on rough tracks (pp 20 and 42) will prepare you for the techniques best suited for driving over rocks and stone. The rough definition applicable here to 'rocks and stone' is that stones are taken to be anything from gravel up to fist-sized stones and rocks are taken to be over fist sized and up to about 20–30 cm high – the maximum permitted by the under body and under-axle dimensions of Land Rover products.

Take every precaution against grounding the vehicle on rock. As usual, use a marshaller when clearances are tight.

Clearances. What you have read about clearance angles and under-axle clearances on p 30 is doubly important in the context of driving over rocks and stones. Getting it slightly wrong on clearances when traversing mud will probably scrape earth from the obstacle and take paint off the underside of the vehicle. Making the same mistake over rocks will likely bring the vehicle to a very abrupt halt and possibly damage components as well. Land Rover products' robustness and resistance to 'battle damage' should be regarded as accident insurance, not part of deliberate everyday driving. Take every precaution to ensure you do not run the vehicle into contact with heavy stones or rocks.

When forced onto limiting rocks for short distances use a marshaller and 1st gear low range. See also photo on p 21.

Tyres. Tyres too are potentially very vulnerable to damage on rocky ground – especially the sidewalls of radial-ply tyres – but this and overall operating costs can be reduced by attention to:

1. Inflation. Be sure the tyres are fully inflated to road pressures before traversing rocky going – even if this means re-inflation after deflating for previous soft ground.

2. Sidewall awareness. The most vulnerable parts of a tyre on rocks are the sidewalls. The best on/off-road tyres are radials but these, with their thinner, flexible sidewalls, are particularly prone to 'bacon-slicer' damage – so-called because the action of the tyre sidewall against an intrusive sharp rock resembles the action of a bacon-slicer. Develop 'sidewall awareness' when driving over rocks.

3. Cross-ply tyres. Where operations are almost exclusively off-road on rock or stone – such as fleet operations in quarries – the more damage-resistant qualities (at full inflation pressures) of cross-ply tyres could help keep operating costs down. It is *essential*, however, to consider and accommodate the following criteria:

a. Virtually all 7.50 x 16 cross-plies are 'L' speed rated (see table p 117), ie limited to 125 kph (75 mph), so should not be fitted to high powered vehicles operating on-road.

b. Cross-ply tyres have higher rolling resistance so will slightly reduce fuel economy.

c. Cross-ply tyres have marginally less grip than radials so handling on-road would be affected.

Stony tracks and plains. Not all your rock/stone traverses will be over on-the-limits boulders. Stony tracks or vast stony plains in the desert will be very much less hazardous. Well inflated tyres and an alertness for potential further hazards, however, will be important. As with corrugations (next spread) braking will be much less efficient on loose stones. See also Section 7, p 108.

On-foot survey, marshalling. All the points mentioned so far point to the need for looking at a difficult rocky stretch or obstacle on foot and then being marshalled across by a helper. This will ensure – since the marshaller can see all eight sidewalls and the under-side of the vehicle and axles – that no damage is done.

Low box control. The relevance of low box and its ability to control the vehicle's forward motion steadily (rather than just make considerable power available) is nowhere more applicable than in traversing large rocks. First gear, low box, clutch fully-in, very low engine speed will enable the vehicle to crawl steadily, without heaving, jerking or lurching, over the very worst rocky terrain.

Cross-ply tyres could lower costs in continuous rock/stone operations. BUT, note speed limitations.

Braking is far less effective on stony going.

On-the-limit rocky going demands 1st gear low range for control.

...continued

Land Rover Experience

Rocks, stones, corrugations – continued

Palliative effects of the 'harmonic' speed applies <u>only</u> to transverse corrugations of the type shown opposite. Irregular obstacles like the boulders shown above can only be taken at a crawl – 1st gear low range – with the foot fully off the clutch and the centre diff lock disengaged. Steering feedback can be sharp, even with power assistance, so thumbs must be kept on and parallel to the rim of the steering wheel. With great care and the use of a marshaller, no damage should result.

Corrugations

Transverse corrugations on track demand a 'harmonic' speed to reduce the vibration on the vehicle.

'Harmonic' speed. A special manifestation of something between stony going and rough or unsurfaced tracks is the phenomenon of transverse corrugations across graded earth, sand or gravel tracks – regular, wave-form undulations that can stretch for tens of kilometres in front of you on remote area routes. The corrugations, also called 'washboard' in America, have a peak-to-peak distance of 0.5 to 1 metre and can be as much as 20 cm deep. They are formed by the action (and harmonics) of the suspension and tyres of the track's major-user vehicles on the soil. This latter is an important point since the technique to adopt when driving over them involves using the natural harmonics of your own vehicle's suspension to minimise the apparent roughness of the ride. There will be a speed of driving – usually between about 40 and 60 kph (25–35 mph) in Land Rover products – where the effect of the corrugations *on the vehicle body* will be minimised. The italics are used as a

The 'harmonic' speed reduces body shake to just-bearable limits but still tortures unsprung components like axles.

reminder that the suspension and un-sprung parts such as the axles are undergoing a rare form of torture over such ground, even though the body and passengers may be (relatively) more comfortable.

Reduced brake effectiveness. An indication of the ordeal of the unsprung components will be clear when enduring

Range Rover travelling at 'harmonic' speed on moderate corrugations (below) reduces jarring on body though suspension still suffers. Remember dramatically reduced steering and brake effectiveness. Travel on such tracks is invariably accompanied by thick dust clouds (below left); on-coming vehicles cause temporary obliteration of the track and passing slower trucks can be hazardous.

the acceleration to these speeds and when decelerating from them. (If you still have any doubts about what the suspension is going through, look out of the driver's window at the front axle.) It is vital to remember also that, since the wheels are virtually jumping from the crest of one corrugation to the next, they are in touch with the ground for a fraction of the time they would normally be. Steering and particularly *braking effectiveness will be dramatically reduced* when going rapidly on corrugated tracks. Driving a Land Rover on a track where the corrugations were formed by, say, a four-ton truck will be especially unpleasant since the suspension harmonics of the truck will not match those of your Land Rover and there will be no 'magic speed' where the ride appears to smooth out.

Dramatic reductions in braking and steering effectiveness take place when driving on corrugated tracks.

WADING

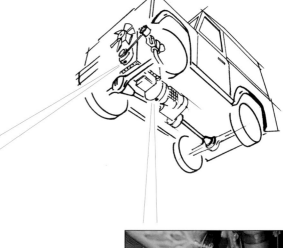

Preparations

Think ahead. Think of wading as a wet, blind and usually cold manifestation of every other type of obstacle and hazard you may come across. This is not meant as an unduly gloomy warning so much as a reminder that the same kind of potential problems can lurk beneath the water as you may see on dry land and that advance knowledge of them is no less important.

The same obstacles can lurk – unseen – under the water as on dry land. Plan, and recce, ahead.

Wading plugs. Other advance knowledge it will pay to acquire well before you get anywhere near a wading situation is the location of the vehicle's wading plugs and how to put them in. All Land Rover products are provided with drain holes in the clutch housing between the engine and gearbox and also (where such a belt is fitted) at the bottom of the camshaft belt drive housing at the front of the engine beneath the fan. These holes are a safety

Always fit the wading plugs. Make the plugs, a 13 mm spanner and a groundsheet part of your standard kit.

feature to ensure that, in the event of an oil leak in these regions, the oil can drain away and not get onto the clutch or cam drive belt. In case of deep wading, however, these holes must first be blocked off by the insertion of screw-in wading plugs. It is convenient to keep these plugs (available from Land Rover dealers) and the appropriate 13 mm (or 1/2" AF) spanner handy within the vehicle. It is important that the plugs be removed after wading – not necessarily at once but within a few days. If a vehicle is used for regular

Land Rover Experience

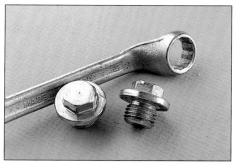

Always take the trouble to walk the stream before committing the vehicle – above, and see diagram p 34. Wading plugs (left) are fitted in clutch housing (photo opposite, right – location above and ahead of chassis cross member) and, if applicable, in the bottom of the cam drive-belt housing (opposite, left – location ahead of the sump; above, and slightly aft of front axle casing).

wading the plugs should be removed, checked for oil leakage and replaced every week or two.

Walking the course. Water obstacles, large or small, should always (as mentioned on p 34, 'Look before you leap') be examined on foot before committing a vehicle. Rubber boots and a long stick are the extras required for an on-foot survey before wading. Generally, stagnant water is more

likely to be a hazard than a river or a stream as flowing water tends to prevent a build-up of silt. The silt in a stagnant pool or mud hollow can be several feet deep. Ensuring that the bottom of the pool or stream is firm enough along all of your proposed traverse is essential and it will inevitably take some time to do thoroughly. Markers may be necessary (such as sticks) to be sure the vehicle follows the route you have proved on foot.

Always walk through first with a stick. Better to get wet legs than have your vehicle stuck in an underwater hollow.

...continued

Wading – continued

Limitations

Wading limitations, how to proceed. The maximum advisable wading depth for Land Rover products is 0.5 metre – about 5-6 cm (a thumb length) below the top of the wheel rim or, perhaps more memorably, 5-6 cm higher than the top of the average rubber boot. Note the implications of this – your brakes will be completely immersed in water but the radiator cooling fan will be clear and so will the exhaust pipe exit – just. Land Rover customers all over the world frequently travel through water where the depth exceeds 0.5 metres. In these conditions the following precautions are advisable:

The normal wading depth limit of 0.5 m runs just beneath the top of the wheel rim, just above the door shut line and about equal to exhaust height.

Normal wading depth limit 0.5 m – just below the top of the wheel rim.

1. Gear and speed. Low box with a gear appropriate to the amount of power and control over rocks required. Keep enough rpm to preclude water entering the exhaust pipe if it is submerged. Speed in general should be low but fast enough to keep a small bow-wave ahead of the bumper and thus reduce the height of the water *behind* the bumper, so keeping water away from the fan. In practice, low box 2nd gear is usually about right.

Not too fast, not too slow – fast enough for a small constant-height bow wave. Probably 2nd low.

2. Keeping the ignition dry. If you are using a petrol engine equipped vehicle it is important to keep the ignition dry. The right bow-wave will help. A sheet of plastic lowered in front of the radiator will stop water cascading straight through and onto the fan – again reducing the chance of spray over the electrics. Additionally an old coat, blanket, sack or other heavy fabric can be draped over the engine behind the fan to keep the harness dry; remember, however, this can be a fire hazard so keep it well clear of the exhaust manifold. *Do not remove the fan belt* as this will stop the water pump and could damage the engine; the sheet of plastic draped in front of the radiator grille will also prevent liquid mud

It is VITAL not to let water near the engine air intake – through splash or any other cause.

from blocking the radiator matrix.

3. Essential – keep engine air intake clear of water. Major damage to engines can result if even small amounts of water get past the air filter and into the cylinders. Never risk this happening. Choose another route where the water depth is less. You may have seen pictures of Land Rover vehicles taking part in the Camel Trophy almost submerged in water but these vehicles will have been specially modified with raised, roof-level air intakes for the engine.

After wading. It is essential to dry your brakes after wading. Whilst still in low

Optimum bow-wave produces dip aft of bumper, keeps water away from fan. Raised air intake permits deeper wading for diesels. Pre-attached tow rope useful precaution. Select air suspension on Range Rovers to high profile.

range, drive a short distance applying the brakes lightly; this will squeegee the discs dry and the heat will dry the pads. Remove any plastic sheeting or other engine protection used for the operation. The wading plugs need not be removed immediately if further wading is envisaged – but see para on p 68 about regular use. Remember your handbrake too will be wet.

Oil contamination. If you regularly undertake wading be aware of the risk of water contamination in the vehicle lubricating oil. This will manifest itself as emulsified oil, easily identified because of its milky appearance. A hot axle case or gearbox plunged into a cold stream for any time will cool suddenly, tending to suck water in through oil seals or breathers. All Land Rover vehicles now have carefully designed remote breathers (long black nylon pipes that vent the transmission casings high in the engine compartment) but periodic checks are still advisable.

Getting stuck, recovery and precautions. Covered fully under the section 'Recovery', p 77, recovery principles remain the same but are complicated by the lower part of the vehicle being under water. Anticipation is the key – such as pre-attachment of a tow rope (or pre-extension of the winch line) so that you do not have to grope with the problem under water.

Squeegee the brakes dry after wading – 20 m or so, low range, against light brake.

Pre-attach tow rope and coil it on bonnet if there is a risk of needing a tow.

Land Rover Experience

ICE AND SNOW

More traction, same brakes

4x4s are better than 4x2s on snow and ice for traction – but remember your braking is very similar.

4x4, 4x2 differences. Most readers of this book will have experience of driving on snow and ice in ordinary cars. Indeed many will have bought a Land Rover product partly because it will give them more reliable transport in wintry conditions. Though traction in snow is best in temperatures below -20° to -30°C and less good between -20°C and freezing point, the basic principles of being very

ABS will give the best possible braking under the prevailing conditions – but cannot change packed snow into dry tarmac.

gentle with both the throttle and the brakes will apply in just the same way on a 4x4 so it is well to establish first just what the differences are between the two types of vehicle:

1. Double the traction.... As we have seen, the 4x4 has double the traction. In snow and ice conditions this should be regarded not as a means of putting twice as much power on the road but as a means of putting the same power on the road spread between twice as many wheels. This asks less of the surface in terms of grip and so you are less likely to get spinning wheels.

2. ...but the same braking. What is often forgotten in the feeling of confidence that a 4x4's tractive performance in snow generates is that the method of stopping is the same as that of any normal car – four wheels on the ground, each one's rotation retarded by brakes. Indeed, 4x4s are generally a lot heavier than normal cars and have a correspondingly increased amount of kinetic energy to arrest. Beware, therefore, of letting your feeling of invincibility extend to the braking department when you are on snow or ice.

3. ABS – very good, but not magic. ABS anti-lock braking will give you *the best braking possible under the circumstances* but will not reverse the laws of physics. The Range Rover's ABS system is one of the best and most versatile there is and it will eliminate the human error of locking the wheels; it will yield the maximum retardation possible from given surface conditions – as well as enormously improving directional control – but it will not turn ice into dry tarmac. The surface conditions are still the limiting factor.

Gentle right foot – again

Driving technique. The driving techniques employed for snow and ice are generally similar to those used for mud or wet grass.

1. High gear. Select the highest gear possible for the conditions. ('**D**' in *Auto*.)

2. Diff lock. Engage the centre differential lock (if manually selected) – and disengage it as soon as non-icy ground is reached.

3. Throttle, brake, steering. Use minimum throttle opening when driving away and accelerating, even if electronic traction control (ETC) is fitted; avoid violent movements of the steering wheel. Drive slowly and brake with great caution to avoid locking the wheels. Cadence braking will help (see p 28, p 100 and Glossary p 148).

.... / **contd**

The same principles apply as for slippery slopes – highest gear possible, gentle and sensitive use of brakes, throttle and steering.

When you have to get through – or even when it would just be convenient – a good 4x4 is only half the battle; the other half is a sensitive driver.

Ice and snow –
continued

*What lies under the
snow? If you are the
first out, it will just
be road.*

Gentle right foot – contd

What lies beneath. As with sand, there
are, of course, a dozen combinations of
criteria affecting snow and ice –
mainly concerned with what lies beneath
the present surface of the snow – that will
extend or reduce the limits of traction of
your vehicle. These cannot be quantified in
any book but they acquire new relevance in
the light of a large-wheeled 4x4:

*Snowfall on top of
compressed snow
will be very slippery.
A classic case for diff
lock in high box.*

1. First on the road? If, as if often the case,
you and your Land Rover are first on the
road after the first snow on untreated
roads, this is the best traction you will get
in snow. Bold and/or sharp treaded M+S
tyres will cut through the soft snow either
to the ground beneath or will make the first
compressed snow 'rails' for you to travel
on. These are as grippy as they will ever be.
Conditions get worse from now on.

*As a 'first on the
road' vehicle hub-
high snow is no
problem. Deeper
than that and with
small drifts, use
momentum laced
with discretion.*

2. Second or later? When others have been
on the roads first, their compressed tracks
will make slippery going and, as you will
have done many times, driving out of the
previous tracks will get fractionally more
traction. As before, 4x4 will give more
traction but no improvement, per se, in
braking. On long descents or hairpin bends
stay in a low gear.

3. Subsequent snowfalls. Snowfall on top
of previous compressed tracks which may
in places have slicked-over into streaks of
pure ice is another well enough known
phenomenon in which a large-wheeled and
heavy 4x4, delicately driven, will prove its
worth in obtaining traction. Braking will be
fractionally better than a car by reason of
the tyre treads but only as long as it is done
gently. Again, cadence braking – see p 28,
p 100 and Glossary p 148 – (if you have no

*Carry a long tow-
rope, shovels, gum
boots to low-box
others out of ditches
and be on your way.*

ABS) will pay dividends and the big
wheels' ability to steer through and
towards snow having no underlying ice
will prove an advantage.
Auto transmission, traction control. Land
Rover vehicles fitted with automatic
transmission, electronic traction control
(ETC) and ABS will be at an advantage in
wintry conditions but these aids to gentler
traction do not invalidate the 'gentle right
foot' driving philosophy.

Snowdrifts. A Land Rover's big wheels,
locked centre diff and appropriate tyres
driven on all four wheels are ingredients
for charging snowdrifts and getting
through. Or they can be ingredients for
getting it wrong and finishing up sitting on
top of a vehicle's length of compressed
snow and having to dig the snow out from
under the vehicle. Do not be too ambitious
with what you attempt to barge through.
Anything above hub depth is starting to
get marginal for sustained travel;
individual small drifts deeper than this can
often be successfully tackled. As ever, the
low box, probably in 2nd or 3rd (with diff
lock), will be the appropriate weapon.

Helping yourself and others. Other traffic
and those inappropriately equipped having
got into trouble will all too frequently be
the cause, in winter conditions, of your not
getting through to your destination despite
your having, without them, the capability
to do so. To free them and yourself from
delays, carrying a long tow rope, shovels,

Off-road snow demands careful sounding – on foot with a stick. On road, with the right tyres, hub-high snow will present little difficulty. On front wheels use only Land Rover approved snow chains.

gumboots, gloves and some kind of under-wheel traction aid (see 'Self-recovery' p 78) will help reduce everyone's problems. Pulling a car from a ditch with this equipment and careful use of the low box and throttle takes only minutes – see 'Recovery – towing out', p 82.

Tyres and tyre pressures. As mentioned already, each type of terrain has an optimum tyre type and whilst your Land Rover can cover a wide variety of terrain, a single set of tyres for such a spread will limit your capability in one or more medium. In general, a mud or M+S (mud and snow) kind of tyre – they will have quite a bold, sharp-edged tread – will be best for use in snow. Use normal road tyre pressures. Details: Section 7 – 'Tyres', p 108.

Snow chains. If you do not have a full set of four snow chains fit the first pair to the front wheels since this will give you grip as well as steering in slippery conditions. To some extent it will also prepare a path for the back wheels. Since a 4x4 has four

driven wheels a second set of chains will be beneficial. If using front snow chains off road *there is a danger, with certain types of chain, that full axle articulation and full steering lock at the same time could enable the chains to damage the front brake pipes.* A new type of chain, more easy to attach, is now available as an approved Land Rover accessory which obviates this danger (Land Rover part numbers RTC9590 for 7.50 x 16 tyres and RTC9589 for 205 x 16 and 6.50 x 16 tyres). See also 'Self-recovery' p 78.

Snow off-road. As there is not a smooth potentially slippery surface beneath it, snow off-road is easier to cope with than snow on tarmac carriageways. A moment's thought, however, highlights the dangers of minor drifting of the snow covering potentially destructive obstacles such as small rock outcrops or gullies on hillsides. The situation is similar to fording streams in that the dangers are hidden; the solution is the same – an on-foot inspection and prodding with a stick in doubtful areas.

Tyres with bold sharp tread patterns are best. Fit only the latest Land Rover approved snow chains.

Off-road snow is generally easier - but probe for hidden obstacles like rocks or ditches.

Land Rover Experience

Land Rover Experience

SECTION 5

OPERATIONS – RECOVERY

SELF-RECOVERY

Traction aids

The calm approach. Having got 'stuck', self-recovery is the art of remedying the situation without the need to call upon outside assistance. The brutal truth is that in most cases getting stuck is a function of driver error – misreading the ground or the obstacle, or not accurately knowing the limitations of your vehicle. Whilst we all try our best with these things and all gradually get better, equally certain is the fact that we all occasionally make mistakes. Admitting this is at least half the battle for it enables you to go about the remedial action in the right spirit – philosophically cheerful acceptance of a minor challenge rather than agitation, embarrassment, bluster or the suspicion that life has just dealt you the ultimate humiliation!

Everyone gets bogged occasionally. Do not take it as a personal slight!

Knowing the problems. It helps to know what problems may be ahead. The categories in which you may find yourself stuck are shown below. Knowing this helps you see the problems coming and avoid them.

Traction – wheels spinning. A given amount of power plus a combination of not enough grip and not enough weight on a wheel can cause it to spin. In these circumstances ETC (Electronic Traction Control – see Glossary), if fitted, will brake the spinning rear wheel. Without ETC, in the case of not enough weight on the wheel (the axle may be at an angle to the chassis and the lower wheel is spinning) see under Articulation overleaf. If grip is the problem in a static re-start case first try a higher gear and a very gentle throttle.

If you've missed the chance to reverse out, admit it, smile and go on to the next stage ....

More grip. If that fails, inserting some gripping medium between the wheel and the ground is the solution – stones, brushwood, mats, baulks of timber or items

...the next stage is digging and the use of something to put under the wheels.

designed especially for the purpose: sand ladders, metal planking and recovery channels. Beware (see sub para 2 below) of anything that can flick up beneath the vehicle and cause damage.

1. Sand ladders can of course be used in any medium – sand, mud, snow – and are specially made aluminium ladders about 1.5 metres long, 35 cm wide and with rungs about 15 cm apart (gripping edges outermost). They are thrust under the front – or rear – of the wheels (if necessary scooping out earth or sand to get them farther in) and the vehicle will find grip on the ladders and haul itself out. If necessary, the ladders are moved round to the front (or rear) of the vehicle a second, third or fourth time to provide further traction in the direction of travel. Sand ladders of the right type – side members 6-7 cm deep – can be used for minor bridging of ditches.

2. Steel planking (PSP – the perforated lengths of interlocking steel planking originally made for WW2 bush airfields) is used in the same way as sand ladders. PSP is heavier and more difficult to use than aluminium sand ladders; it is too flexible to be used for bridging (and can bend upward to snag the underside of the vehicle) but is excellent for laying over logs or branches to provide a vehicle trackway. Despite the contradiction in terms, PSP is sometimes available in aluminium.

3. Recovery channels. These combine the best aspects of sand ladders with a third of the bulk. They are in effect a pair of purpose-built aluminium alloy grip panels 1.5 metres by 35 cm, each cut into three equal lengths and joined with nylon rope – large photo opposite. The articulation afforded by the rope links makes them easier to push in front of the wheels without – as is the case with ladders or PSP – the danger of the remainder of the unit fouling the vehicle chassis. Best of all, when you have finished with them, the

Land Rover Experience

*The same principles apply to use of
traction aids in mud or dry sand. Use
them before the situation gets too bad
and dig sufficient space for them to
work first time.*

three sections can be folded up, bagged
and stowed within the vehicle. (At present
these items are only made and available
from Barong, F.92370 Chaville, France.)

Flotation – sinking in soft ground.
Although technically there is a difference
between a lack of traction and a lack of
flotation, in practice the two usually strike
together and a joint solution – use of

reduced tyre pressures (see Section 7,
'Tyres' p 108) and/or load spreaders such
as sand ladders etc mentioned above – will
be the answer. If no load spreaders are
carried, branches or brushwood should be
used. If sinkage is considerable so that the
vehicle is hung up (see next paragraph)
digging to remove the obstacle or jacking
to permit the channels to be put under the
wheels will be necessary.

*Use shovels early to
save a wheel-
spinning bogging
getting worse. Invest
an extra few
minutes' digging
and get out first
time.*

Always dig away in front of a wheel before
inserting the sand tracks. This helps
ensure first-time extraction.

...continued

Land Rover Experience

Self-recovery – continued

Digging, recovery tools

Digging the ground away from under a vehicle hung-up on the chassis provides good motivation for not letting it happen again. As ever, if in doubt use a marshaller.

Avoid under belly hang-up on ridges and rocks – can be damaging. Recovery awkward, time consuming.

Under-vehicle obstacles – hung-up on ridges or rocks. Least forgivable of driver-inflicted situations, especially if you have a passenger with you who could have got out and marshalled you over the obstacle, getting the chassis hung up on ridges or rocks is also the most potentially damaging. The price will be paid, however, since the only way out of this predicament (unless you have a high-lift bumper jack – see 'Recovery tools' below and diagram/photo opposite) is actually to dig the obstacle away from under the vehicle with a shovel. It will be difficult using the shovel at full arm's length under the vehicle and in addition the vehicle will be tending initially to collapse down onto the shovel as it is used. Knowing what is involved and having the patience to do it slowly but surely will unfailingly get you out of this situation. If it is immovable rock and you are hung up with the centre of the chassis on it the situation is more serious but jacking front or rear to put packing under the wheels will achieve a recovery just as reliably.

Exceeding articulation limits is a common way of becoming immobilised. Dig under the 'high' wheels or pack under the 'low' ones.

Articulation – diagonal wheels in the air. As we have seen ('Ridges and ditches', p 46) it is possible to get a vehicle immobilised by misjudging the amount of axle articulation involved in crossing a ridge or ditch diagonally. (An axle is on full articulation when one wheel is pushed up into the wheel arch as far as it will go and the other wheel is hanging down as far as it will go.) A very common manifestation is 'the diagonal tightrope' in which, say, the rear offside wheel and front nearside wheel are both on full bump and the complementary wheels are hanging down – with the axle differentials permitting the hanging-down wheels to spin when you apply power. This situation

For planned off-roading, carry a full self-recovery kit.

will stop you but has a very straightforward solution – either pack up beneath the spinning wheels or dig away beneath the full bump wheels. It is difficult to get earth packed in tightly enough under the hanging wheels (though inserting a sand ladder, levering up and packing with rocks can work) so almost invariably digging under the hung up wheels is the solution. As with the case above, the vehicle is trying to collapse on your shovel as you dig but, again, patience will invariably win the day.

Recovery tools. If you are planning a journey in which off-roading and the risk of getting stuck exists, the following equipment is worth taking:

> Rubber boots, gloves, overalls.
> Electric tyre pump for re-inflation of tyre.
> Two shovels (pointed blades, not square ends like spades).
> 2 tow ropes (totalling 25 metres) and appropriate end fittings.
> Articulated sand channels or sand ladders – see previous page.
> Hi-lift jack – if appropriate to the vehicle (see below).
> Baulk of timber about 30 x 20 x 5 cm to put under foot of hi-lift or other jack to prevent sinkage.

Hi-lift jack is a valuable recovery tool but must be used with strict adherence to safety instructions – including use of diff lock. Unless bumpers on Range Rover and Discovery are modified, it can only be used on Defender (below and far right). Bottle-jack with shovel and timber baulks can be used in similar fashion on wheel or hub. Use wood 'cushion' on alloy wheel rims.

Hi-lift jack can be used to raise a vehicle out of deep ruts and 'lateral pole-vault' it onto easier ground.

Hi-lift jack. As the sketch shows, the hi-lift jack is a mechanical bumper jack capable of a lift of a metre or more. A Defender, for instance, that has been run into deep ruts and is unable to get out could have the front end physically lifted out of the ruts and, by then pushing the jack over sideways, could be 'pole-vaulted' onto more suitable ground. Equally, the front end can also be lifted to insert ladders or branches under the wheels. Hi-lift jacks are very effective in operation – one can also be converted into a hand winch – but are very heavy and awkward to carry; additionally,

as bumper jacks they require the square section of the Defender bumper and are not suitable to use on a Range Rover or Discovery – unless special bumper modifications are done. If you have an operating spectrum in which a hi-lift jack would be a useful recovery tool, it would be worth making modifications to enable it to be carried in a rack and used on appropriate sockets on the vehicle.

Hi-lift jack – safety. Pay special attention to safety when using a hi-lift jack. As a 'mono-pod' it is inherently unstable and hand-brake, diff-lock and wheel chocks should be used to prevent the vehicle rolling forward or back. *Do not leave the jack unless the operating handle is in the vertical position.*

Winch. Unless required for operating in particular conditions, a winch is expensive and heavy to have as a 'just-in-case' recovery aid. When trying to co-ordinate it with power from driven wheels it is slow in operation, but provided there is something to winch onto – it can work wonders in certain self-recovery situations. See p 90.

Hi-lift jack versatile, effective, needs care in use – plus brake, diff-lock, chocks.

RECOVERY – TOWING OUT

Ropes and attachments

Second-vehicle safety; long ropes. Where conditions are likely to be close to the limits of your Land Rover's capabilities, you are strongly advised not to go off-roading without a second vehicle. As this and the next spread will show, the potential for recovery where one vehicle is able to help another is a considerable improvement on the situation of a solo vehicle trying self-recovery. Firstly, always use a *long* towing rope – better still a combination of two that make up a long rope. That way the towing vehicle will not be in the same bog or soft sand that has stopped the first one. As with any rope, do not let it tangle round axles.

Tow rope attachment points – vehicle. Tow rope attachment to the towing vehicle should naturally be at the towing hitch if one is fitted. This uses the longitudinal chassis members and the rear cross member to provide a load-spreading attachment point. At the front and rear of all Land Rover vehicles, beneath the chassis, lashing points – two front and two rear – are fitted, principally for securing vehicles on trailers. If a tow hitch is not fitted these can be used (as pairs, not singly) for towing. Better still, and designed to cope with far higher loads, extra-strong lashing/towing rings (Land Rover part no RRC3237) can be fitted in lieu of the normal lashing rings at the same chassis points (lower left photo opposite).

Use a bridle and two attachment points. The standard lashing points are designed for loads less than maximum towing loads but can be used for normal recovery towing (not snatch towing – see next section) if both eyes are used with a long

Take a second vehicle for safety and to assist recovery if you are going off-roading.

Use – and prepare – a long tow rope. If you have no towing hitch, use BOTH lashing eyes and a bridle.

Preparation of tow ropes should include U-bolts and shackle pins.

NEVER loop tow rope round the rear axle of a Land Rover vehicle – it could damage the brake pipes.

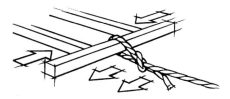

Attached at mid point, tow rope will bend a weak bumper, drawing chassis members together. Move rope close to bumper attachment points.

Too short a towing bridle will have same effect – also putting extreme strain on bridle rope.

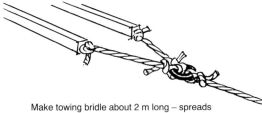

Make towing bridle about 2 m long – spreads load without any 'pinching' component.

bridle – a rope attached to both lashing eyes and joined to the main tow rope two or three metres away of the vehicle. (Do not make this bridle less than two metres in length and do make it of a rope to each lashing ring rather than a single loop through both rings. This way you will minimise rope tension and also eliminate any tendency to draw the chassis members together – see diagram.) Never put a tow rope round a bumper since this will lead to the rope being cut by the bumper's sharp

U-bolt and pin is reliable, repeatable way of attaching ropes. Standard tow hitch cleared for 3500 kg (upper right). If not fitted, use long bridle on lashing eyes or RRC3237 shackles (above and right).

edge. Nor should a rope be put round an axle since this involves the virtual certainty of damaging brake pipes.

Tow rope ends. Ensuring that your tow ropes have properly prepared ends is a very worthwhile precaution. Few things can add so effectively to the problems of having to extract a bogged vehicle than finding that tow ropes have to be knotted round tow points and then need a marlin spike in order to undo the knot afterwards.

Spliced-in metal eyes and the use of U-bolts and shackle pins on properly prepared ropes makes the exercise extremely simple and quick. If you do not have a tow hitch at both ends of the vehicle, prepare a suitable length of rope with U-bolts at each end to pick up on the lashing eyes and act as a two metre bridle onto which the main tow-rope can be attached. The main tow rope should be similarly prepared for your particular vehicle.

Ideally don't use bumpers for towing; most bumpers cut tow ropes. In emergency pad with sacking, move rope close to attachment bolts.

...continued

Land Rover Experience

Recovery – towing out – continued

Co-ordinated recovery

Meaning, procedure. The implications of a co-ordinated recovery are that the power and traction of both vehicles – even though one of them, being stuck, has a limited capability – are used together at the moment when the tow is undertaken. This is a commonsense point but all too often, in the stress of a vehicle becoming bogged, the point is forgotten and spinning wheels and slack, then jerking tow-ropes become the ingredients of minor confusion. A helpful sequence aide-memoire for a normal assisted recovery would be as follows:

1. Marshaller, co-ordinator. Ingredients of a co-ordinated recovery: one stuck vehicle, one recovery (towing) vehicle, appropriate – long – tow ropes, two drivers and a third person to act as marshaller and co-ordinator.

2. Take your time. If the stuck vehicle is hung up on an obstacle invest five or ten minutes in some spade work to make sure the first extraction attempt is the one that works. Even if there is no digging, still take your time.

3. Backwards best? Towing out backwards is sometimes a more reliable option. At least the stuck vehicle has wheel tracks leading to its present position. In this case, with the vehicles back-to-back during recovery, a second marshaller standing in 'front' of the stuck vehicle is useful to keep that driver in the picture by relaying the hand signals of the principal marshaller ahead of the tug. As with reversing back down a hill (see p 50), the driver of the stuck vehicle should keep both hands on the steering wheel to preclude steering 'runaway' during recovery.

4. Towing vehicle clear. Position the towing vehicle so that it is well clear of the conditions that bogged the first vehicle (a long rope is almost invariably more use than a short one for this reason), attach the rope to both vehicles, position the third person so that both drivers can easily see him and have him marshal the towing vehicle forward until the rope is tight.

5. Visual signals, simultaneous clutches. Decide on the gear to be used – not necessarily 1st low box; 2nd could well be better – have both vehicles start engines, engage gear and wait for the signal from the marshaller for both drivers to engage the clutch. As with all marshalling, (see also 'Marshalling', p 34) this should be a visual not a spoken signal: a raised arm to instruct both drivers to be ready and in gear, raised arm describing small circles to instruct them to rev the engines, then drop the raised arm to instruct them to engage the clutches.

6. Marshaller in control. The marshaller should move backwards as the vehicles move towards him, still controlling the operation and being ready to give an immediate STOP signal if he sees any problems. He is the only one who can properly judge how the recovery is going. He too can judge when it is done; he can signal the lead vehicle to stop and the now mobile towed one to come forward slightly to slacken off the rope before disconnecting.

Use a long tow rope and a marshaller to control the operation. Take your time.

Marshaller should use only visual signals to co-ordinate both vehicles' power.

WARNING. When tow starts, NO-ONE should be anywhere near the tow rope.

If stuck vehicle is heavy or badly mired a tandem-tow, carefully co-ordinated, will usually achieve first-time results.

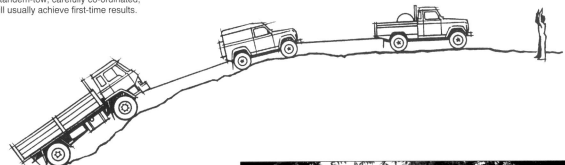

A third-man marshaller is invaluable (right) to ensure clutches of both vehicles are engaged at the same time. A fourth, 'relay', marshaller (left) is useful in a reverse tow.

Safety – the danger of breaking ropes. A tow rope breaking whilst under strain can be lethal or inflict serious injury. *No bystanders or crew should be allowed near a tow rope during the actual tow.* Four to five metres is usually a safe distance but the danger area varies with the length of rope and the techniques used – see 'Recovery – snatch towing', p 86. A breaking rope recoils with whiplash violence. Adequately strong tow ropes are essential as well as rigidly enforced safety procedures in their use.

Pull required. As a guide, the pull required to move a vehicle (as a proportion of its total weight – ie including payload) assuming level ground, is given below:

> Hard metalled road – about 5% of total vehicle weight.
> Grass – about 15%.
> Hard wet sand, gravel, soft wet sand – about 15-20%.
> Sand – soft, dry, loose – about 25-30%
> Shallow mud – about 33%.
> Bog, marsh, clinging clay – about 50%.

Rule-of-thumb. It makes sense that the rope to keep in the back of your Land Rover is the worst-case rope – the one for marsh/bog/clay. Allowing a safety margin to account for unseen damage to the rope and other exigencies it should have a quoted breaking strain about equal to the laden weight of your vehicle. For example, a 14 mm 3-strand polypropylene rope has a breaking strain – when new and undamaged – of 2.79 tonnes (quoted breaking strains are governed by British Standards in the UK) which would be an appropriate *minimum* for all except a laden Defender 110 or 130. For details of laden weights of all Land Rover products see Section 7, 'Technical Data', p126 et seq.

Use a tow rope with a breaking strain about equal to the weight of the vehicle.

WARNING. Breaking tow ropes can be lethal. Regularly inspect for damage. Keep bystanders away.

Land Rover Experience

RECOVERY – SNATCH-TOWING

WARNING. Snatch towing can involve very high forces and is a potentially dangerous procedure. Use only the fixtures and ropes of the kind specified below with methods to ensure loads in the rope and towing fixtures do not exceed 3.4 tonnes – a figure allowing essential safety factors. Ropes, towing fixtures and their attachment areas on the vehicles must be in sound mechanical condition without rust or physical damage. Only the procedure outlined on these pages can be recommended; use it only for vehicle recovery, not on static objects such as tree stumps.

Small, strictly limited, amount of momentum can help recover stuck vehicle.

Vital criteria

Using 'stretch' energy and momentum. Stretching an elastic rope is a means of storing energy. Using vehicle acceleration and then momentum – two different entities here – to effect that stretch is a means of achieving a higher towing pull to recover a bogged-down vehicle than would be achieved by traction alone. The momentum (or more accurately the Kinetic Energy or KE) is stored in the rope and added to the vehicle's tractive effort.

Two types of force. Total pull on the rope derives from:

1. Traction. Traction between the ground and the wheels of the towing vehicle - theoretical maximum around 1.73 tonnes on dry concrete (Defender 90, Tdi, 205 x 16 tyres, 2nd gear low ratio).

NEVER exceed permitted 'step-back'. Table shows examples. Towing attachments MUST be in first class condition.

2. Kinetic energy. Any KE the towing vehicle has at the time the rope goes taut.

The concept of operation outlined here is that the sum of the above must never exceed 3.4 tonnes. If traction is good, KE must be limited; if the towing vehicle is on mud, KE can be allowed to rise to keep the sum at 3.4 tonnes.

Why 3.4 tonnes? This is the factored maximum load, in snatch towing conditions, to be applied to a pair 'JATE rings' part no RRC3237 (see below).

Special ropes only. ONLY nylon ropes specifically designed for this procedure should be used – *with the manufacturer's recommendations.* Snatch towing with chain, steel or other inextensible rope will result in major structural damage to both vehicles involved due to shock loading.

Inherent danger. The potential dangers of snatch towing cannot be over-emphasised. Although widely practised on an *ad hoc* basis, few operators are aware of just how high are the forces involved. Some currently practiced procedures incur tensions in excess of 13 tonnes – *enough to tear out towing attachments with explosive force and lethal potential* – see photo opposite. This, not rope breakage, is the main hazard.

Essential criteria. Consider:
   Specification of rope used.
   Weight of *towing* vehicle.
   Speed of towing vehicle.
   Strength of towing attachments.
Note that the weight of the vehicle being towed is immaterial. Whatever is stuck may be stuck fast – whatever its weight – so the rope and procedure has to cope with an 'immovable' load.

Twin rope attachment points. Use a bridle on both vehicles plus safety lanyards (from the eye of the rope) attached respectively to the front and rear trailer hitches – see photo. The safety lanyard will restrain any hardware coming lose.

Attachment points. These should only be military specification Land Rover towing shackles ('JATE rings': part number RRC3237) – on both vehicles.

Rope specification. *Use only ropes developed specifically for snatch or kinetic energy recovery.* The table below refers to a one-off test on a rope of the following specification:

> Identification: Yellow colour (polyurethane coating) with marker yarn.
> Construction: 24 mm diameter, multiplait nylon.
> *Ultimate* breaking strain 12 tonnes.
> Length: 8 metres with formed, sheathed end eyes *and 20 mm safety lanyards.*
> Attachment bridles: 6 metre yellow 18 tonne roundslings supplied.

Weight and speed of towing vehicle. The particular rope above would be suitable for all Land Rover products from an unladen Defender 90 (1645 kg) to a laden Defender 130 acting as towing vehicle but speed at the point of snatch – here catered for by the amount of 'step-back' from the taut rope condition – must be lower for the heavier vehicle.

Procedure – keep people clear

1. Attach ropes and safety lanyards as indicated above. Drive towing vehicle (tug) slowly forward until rope is taut. As with normal towing, keep people clear of rope.

2. 'Step back'. Reverse tug an appropriate distance to avoid exceeding 3.4 tonnes load – see examples in table below.

3. Using (only) 2nd gear, low ratio, accelerate strongly to extract stuck vehicle.

4. If stuck vehicle does not move, do not exceed a rope stretch beyond normal length (on the rope specified here) of more than 22% - about two paces on the ground with this rope. This stretch represents 3.4 tonnes pull – a useful cross-check.

Life of the rope, storage, care. A nylon KE rope has a finite fatigue life depending on the load to which it is subjected. It must be kept clean, free from grit and sand or other sources of abrasion and not be stored in direct sunlight. It should be stored, dry, in a close-weave, breathable canvas bag.

ONLY specifically designed snatch-tow ropes should be used for this purpose - using manufacturer's load criteria. These ropes are not widely available. Do not be tempted to improvise.

Keep nylon snatch-tow ropes clean, dry, out of sunlight. They have a fatigue life dependent on load.

Maximum 'step-back' from taut 8 metre rope (specified above) to not exceed 3.4 tonnes pull Assumes 2nd gear, low ratio, strong acceleration			
Vehicle type and load	Dry concrete	Dry grass	Wet grass/mud
1. Defender 90, unladen	Zero step-back. Rope sags 100 mm*	1.5 metres	2 metres
2. Defender 130, laden	Do not attempt. Will cause overload	1.8 metres	2.3 metres

Note: The tension achieved in the rope is extremely sensitive to the amount of 'step-back' combined with the type of traction surface you are operating on. It is essential that the safety limits inherent with the 3.4 tonne maximum pull are not infringed. Interpolate between values shown above both for vehicle weight and traction conditions.
* **Only** unladen Defender 90 (ie low mass vehicle) suited to dry concrete, strong acceleration case with this rope.

WINCHING

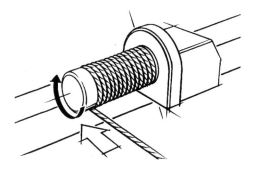

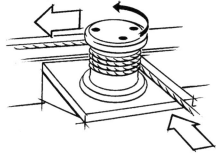

Capstan winch (above). Mechanical drive direct from crankshaft or power take-off shaft. Low geared, operates from idling engine. Uses 20 mm Terylene or Polyester rope. **Drum winch** (left). Electrical (or may be hydraulic). Geared, HD electric motor takes up to 350 amps. 8–9.5 mm wire rope.

Concepts

Be sure a winch is what you need before fitting one.

Weighty decision. Winching is comprehensively covered in a Land Rover Directory publication, 'Winching in Safety'. You are advised to read this book in detail before purchasing or operating a winch. Give careful thought to the implications of a winch before buying. In general they are expensive and heavy, sometimes requiring special front springs for the vehicle and, for preference, fitment of a second battery where an electric winch is involved – further increasing weight; they require special care – and are slow – in operation. But this latter may well be what you want: there are many applications for this alone – the slow controlled pull of a boat from the water or of heavy tree trunks. But for recovering other vehicles you will find most occasions are better catered for by towing with a rope; using a winch to recover a stuck vehicle makes it hard to coordinate the slow speed of the winch with power from the stuck vehicle's own engine. On the other hand, if your business includes recovering passenger cars from ditches or the like, the slow speed and precise controllability of a winch may be what you need.

Electric drum winches not well suited to continuous use. Capstan winches best for continuous heavy duty work.

Approved winches. You are strongly advised to consult your Land Rover supplier when buying a winch and to buy only winches supplied through Land Rover Parts. These will have been approved for your vehicle and the accessories kit will have been specifically engineered for it. Winches may be ordered factory-fitted. Additionally there will be a small Handbook of Winching Techniques issued with the winch which will summarise how to prepare and operate the unit. The following two pages cannot deal with the subject comprehensively.

Winch types. There are two generic classifications of winch:

1. Drum winches comprise a drum rotating about a horizontal axis parallel to the bumper and use 8–9.5 mm wire rope stored on, and spooled onto, the drum. They are usually driven electrically though there are some available with mechanical or hydraulic drive for continuous heavy duty operation.

2. Capstan winches consist of a bollard – like a giant cotton reel – rotating about a

Main photo shows indirect pull electrical winching with cable through pulley block – see next page. Note use of strap to preclude damage to tree bark and that the winching vehicle (right) is square-on to the direction of initial pull. Capstan winch (top) powers rope looped round capstan. Heavy duty electrical Superwinch (left) mounted in bumper also incorporating front trailer hitch – see also p 40.

Winch equipment available for your vehicle specifically approved by Land Rover.

vertical axis. Such winches do not store any rope; they function by moving appropriate ropes – usually 20 mm Terylene/polyester or polypropylene – which have been looped two or three times round the bollard and tensioned on the out-feed side. Capstan winches are mechanically or hydraulically driven and are suitable for continuous heavy duty work.

Casual or heavy duty. Winching can be 'casual' – towing a boat out of the water or the occasional use for self recovery – or

'heavy duty' which implies regular continuous use, usually for professional purposes such as logging or cable laying. Electric winches are not normally suitable for continuous heavy duty use; very high amperages are involved, considerable heat is generated and very high charge rates from the alternator are required. A mechanically driven capstan winch is an altogether more relaxed concept which operates directly from the engine at tick-over; it can thus be used all day without mechanical stress.

Land Rover Experience

Winching – continued

Techniques overview

Which winch. The main planned uses of
the winch will dictate the type fitted as
covered on the previous pages. Actual pull
or cable load should then be considered
too. For vehicle recovery, a rough guide to
the pull required is 1/25th of vehicle gross
weight on tarmac and, for off-road
surfaces, from grass through sand, gravel,
shallow mud to bog or clay, tension
required will be 1/7th to 1/2 vehicle gross
weight – see also p 85. This is well within
the capacity of most winches. Beware,
though, of the steep-slope component of
weight – gross weight times slope angle in
degrees divided by 60. A slope of 15°
(divided by 60) thus adds 1/4 of the
vehicle weight to the pull.

Protect trees. Living trees are likely to be
involved as anchors. Putting a cable round
an unprotected trunk will cut the bark and
'ring-bark' the tree and kill it. For this
reason always use a tree strap – available
as a winching accessory through Land
Rover Parts – or use baulks of timber or
other protection for the bark.

Other anchors. Anchoring the winching
vehicle itself will often be necessary. This
can be done by back-anchoring with rope
to a tree behind it or by the use of ground
anchors – folding heavyweight angle-iron
'chocks' placed in front of the front wheels
and chained to the bumpers. Other ground
anchors to winch onto in the case of self-
recovery (or as back-anchors) can be
effected by use of iron stakes hammered
into the ground. This ironware is heavy
and needs proper stowage but would be
appropriate to carry with you where a
specific winching operation is envisaged.

Buried spare wheel. In extreme conditions
where there is nothing to winch onto and
self-recovery is needed, the vehicle's spare

*Ground anchors (top) prevent winching
vehicle sliding forward when hauling heavy
loads (diagram opposite top). Winch cable
looped through split pulley block and back to
vehicle bumper doubles effective pull of
winch. Pulley can be used for indirect pull –
photo p 89.*

wheel may be buried with the winch cable
attached. The hole must be deep and a 'saw
slot' for the cable allowed; not
recommended in desert conditions.

Safety paramount – breaking cables.
Safety is paramount; breaking cables and
ropes are extremely hazardous. Never step
over a cable under tension and ensure no-
one is close to it when winching is in
progress. Wire cables as used on drum
winches flail laterally when they break so
are particularly dangerous.

Use gloves. Steel cables can have small
broken strands along their length; use thick

Pulley doubles winch maximum 'power' for moving obstacles

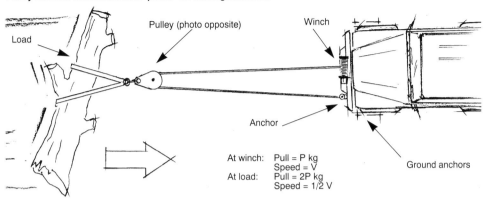

Load

Pulley (photo opposite)

Winch

Anchor

Ground anchors

At winch: Pull = P kg
              Speed = V
At load: Pull = 2P kg
              Speed = 1/2 V

Pulley reduces line strain in self-recovery

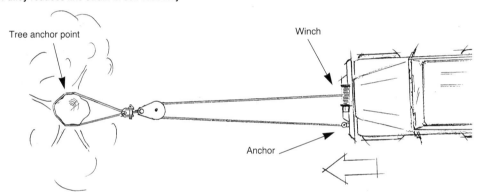

Tree anchor point

Winch

Anchor

winching gloves to protect your hands. The same gloves will be useful for the handling of capstan winch ropes too.

Control cable safety. Be particularly careful that the electrical winch control cable is kept safely clear of the winch cable. The consequences of it becoming caught up in the winch could produce a short circuit making the winch unstoppable without disconnecting the control wire.

Directing – or doubling – the pull. Unlike the bulk and weight of ground anchors, split pulley blocks (photo facing page) are light and small and worth carrying at all times with extra straps and ropes. They are invaluable as a means of producing an indirect pull (photo p 89) or, like a low range transfer gearbox, for producing double the pull at half speed.

Care of cables and ropes. Drum winch cables should spool onto the drum evenly and will do so if the pull is at the correct angle. If there are signs of it not doing so, stop the winching, pay out the cable and spool back onto the drum guiding it by (gloved) hands. Inspect and clean cables and ropes regularly; excessive mud will get into the strands or fibres and cause damage.

Pulley is invaluable 'carry always' accessory to double or direct pull.

Always use thick leather gloves when handling winch cables.

SECTION 6

ADVANCED DRIVING

HIGH/LOW RANGE OVERLAP

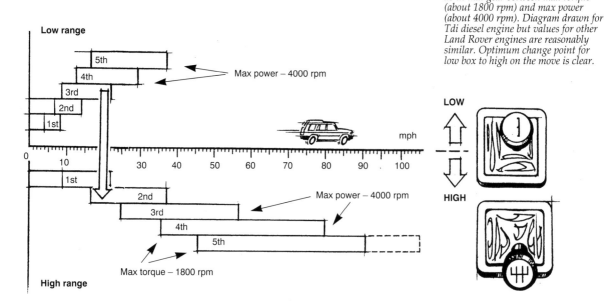

Each bar represents the speed you can do in that gear between max torque (about 1800 rpm) and max power (about 4000 rpm). Diagram drawn for Tdi diesel engine but values for other Land Rover engines are reasonably similar. Optimum change point for low box to high on the move is clear.

Speeds in the gears

Low range is not just extra-low gearing. It overlaps high range to let you choose best overall gearbox span.

High/low range overlap – your choice.
You will see if you study the gear ratios data – and the diagram above – that there is some overlap between low range and high range – for example 4th gear low is roughly equivalent to 2nd gear high so that a given piece of ground could be covered equally well in either. You will frequently find, however, that being in low range rather than the high will give you the ability to tackle sudden track deteriorations such as road washouts or obstacles, without having to carry out a range change. (See also 'Low range – when and how', Section 2, p 20.)

Low to high – moving (manual)

Changing from low to high on the move – without clunks – is well worth learning.

Low to high change – when you need it.
As already shown there are times when it is very useful to be able to start your Land Rover in low range and, once you are moving, continue in high. Typical

examples of this are towing a heavy trailer on hard roads (Section 4, p 38), towing a trailer off-road (this Section, p 102) or just starting the vehicle in marginal traction conditions such as soft sand or mud where it would be risky, once moving, to stop in order to re-select high range.

Low/high change – what gear, what speed.
We have seen from the previous section that there is an overlap between low range and high range so theoretically you could change across from low to high from 3rd, 4th or 5th. In practice it is best to get the vehicle properly moving – say 20-25 mph – before doing a range change; that way, momentum will keep you going when you execute the change. The diagram also shows that the speed/rpm band between max torque and max power nicely suits a 3rd low to 2nd high change. Naturally before contemplating a change from low range to high you should also be sure that conditions are suitable for sustained travel in high range since to change back again you will have to stop.

3rd low to 2nd high on the move – procedure. As the diagram opposite shows, 3rd low is roughly equivalent to 2nd high in terms of road and engine speed. Given the max torque and max power rpm vs speed in the two gears, the range change will have to be made fairly briskly but need not be hurried.

1. Start off in 1st or 2nd low range, accelerate through the gears until you are doing 20-25 mph in 3rd gear, low range.

2. With the main gear lever still in 3rd, double-de-clutch the transfer lever towards you from low to high range, ie depress the clutch and move the transfer lever into neutral. (Note, this will need a short, sharp action with a definite halt at the mid-point of the lever's range of movement.) Clutch down again and move the transfer lever all the way into the HIGH position.

3. With the clutch still depressed, move the main gear lever from 3rd into 2nd gear – towards you again, and across. As the engine was losing rpm whilst you moved the transfer lever, you will find you will need a blip of throttle to raise engine revs to the right level for 2nd gear, high range at 20 mph. Continue in high range 2nd and on up through the gears. Retain or de-select centre diff-lock as required (Defender and Discovery).

High to low on the move? No. This can be done under certain conditions to demonstrate driving skill but there is little practical application. Deteriorating heavy going is when you might need this change and here the time taken to execute it will be enough for the speed to have decayed to nothing. Make life easy; always change to low range when stationary, or easier still, just before the vehicle comes to a halt and with the main gear lever still in a gear.

Automatics. Similar procedures can be carried out with automatic transmission. See next spread – pp 96-99.

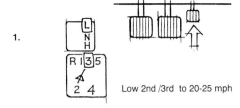

1.

Low 2nd /3rd to 20-25 mph

Low to high – do it from 25 mph in 3rd low. Seems complex to read but is simple to do.

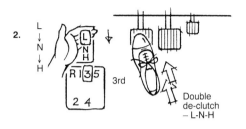

2.

3rd

Double de-clutch – L-N-H

Practise it first on hard roads, then off-road. Momentum decay will be different.

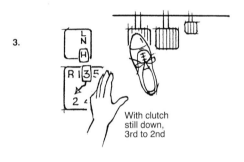

3.

With clutch still down, 3rd to 2nd

Do not bother trying high to low on the move. Stop to make the change.

Classic situation for low-to-high change on the move – softish sand, hard to start in but which, moving, you can take in high range. More usual example, nearer home, is trailer towing – hill starts or moving off from traffic lights.

AUTOMATIC TRANSMISSION

Controlling the automatics

Automatic transmission off-road. Though traditionally most off-road operations are carried out by vehicles with manual transmission, this is no more than a fact of statistics rather than validating any preferences. That there is considerable benefit in the use of automatic transmission off-road is attested by the fact that major power and other military users specify it in their general service vehicles.

Advantages and disadvantages. Whilst the most obvious advantage of auto transmission is that of ease of operation for the driver – important for the military or public utilities user whose mind will be on other things as well as driving – there are also significant benefits in terms of vehicle durability and protection from driver mis-use and transmission shock loads. Off-road performance can itself be enhanced by an automatic's quick seamless changes of gear in 'lift-off' situations – see opposite. The only disadvantages are higher initial cost and increased brake wear though, as already indicated, major professional users with cost-effectiveness in mind compare this with the higher maintenance and repair costs of mis-used manual vehicles and still opt for automatic.

Operating philosophies – knowledge still needed. A Discovery or Range Rover with auto transmission can be operated on a minimum knowledge basis by, say, a fleet or pool operator with disparate drivers of differing experience and for these a basic knowledge will suffice. On the other hand refinement of operating effectiveness and vehicle capability will result if time is taken to learn to get the best from the system.

Basic knowledge. Adherence to Driver's Manual techniques will ensure competent, non-damaging performance from an auto vehicle off road which can be summed up briefly:

1. The automatic gearbox is a ZF four-speed unit with automatic lock-up on 4th ratio above a certain speed to minimise torque converter slippage.

2. 'D' enables (ie permits the use of) all four forward ratios. '3' enables the lower three – ie it will use 1st, 2nd and 3rd but not change above 3rd. Similarly '2' and '1' enable, respectively, 1st and 2nd and then 1st-only.

3. Select 'N' on the main gear selector before moving the transfer lever. If it will not immediately engage, apply the brakes, engage 'D' briefly, go back to 'N' and try again. See p 98 for low transfer to high box on the move.

4. If you are stationary for any length of time, engine running, select 'P' or 'N' rather than let the vehicle idle 'in-gear' which will unecessarily heat up the transmission fluid.

5. If you are in 'P' or 'N' apply the footbrake before selecting a forward or reverse ratio to avoid creep.

Changing to low range, select 'N' on main selector before moving transfer lever. Perusal of overall gear ratios on auto (pp 141, 145), explains why an automatic needs low range 1st for adequate down-slope retardation. For 'up and over' (right) use low range '3' for climb but slip into '1' for descent. For slippery 'forest floor' (above) low 3rd is best (see below) – with diff locked on Discovery.

Gradability vs engine braking. Compared with a manual transmission, you will find an auto has surprising gradability in high range but, particularly off-road, engine braking is inherently poor even in low range. You will need to engage '1' low range to obtain satisfactory engine braking on a descent. Note that if speed is too high this will not engage, even though it has been selected – see next paragraph.

Steep up and down. A steep climb followed by a steep descent sums this situation up well. Whilst you will probably be able to climb well enough in high box on 'D', you will need low box '1' for the descent. To save doing a range change at the top of the incline the technique should thus be to engage low transfer before the obstacle, select '3' (see below why), make the ascent and, at the top, with forward speed at a minimum, pull the main selector back to '1' in order to get maximum retardation for the descent. If you are over the summit and select '1' with the speed too high, it will not engage; you will stay in 2nd or 3rd with little or no engine braking – see p 100 for emergency procedure.

'Lift-off' elimination of wheel-spin. The reason for selecting '3' before a slippery ascent or other potential wheel-spin situation is that as soon as the wheels begin to spin the auto sensors will recognise the reduced torque and change up; this will tend to eliminate wheel-spin as soon as it occurs – in just the same way as you would lift off the throttle with a manual transmission to quench wheel-spin near the top of a steep loose slope. Not selecting 'D' ensures change-up is not too high.

Muddy, 'forest floor' situations. The same applies for 'forest floor' slippery mud situations. Even though the main ratio actually in use may be 1st or 2nd, having the selector in '3' ensures that, as soon as wheel-spin and its reduced torque is sensed, the gearbox will change up to 3rd to eliminate spin.

The main off-road control you will use with auto is aimed at improving down-slope retardation.

Auto will change up to low-box 3rd on a loose slope better than you could on a manual. Use the facility and save wheel-spin.

...continued

Automatic transmission – continued

To tow a dead-engine automatic with all four wheels on the ground, unlock steering and put both gear levers into 'N'. (See driver's manual for details of lifted tow and prop-shaft disconnect). Tow-starting is not possible.

Low to high – moving (auto)

Low to high range on the move is easier to do well on an auto than on a manual.

On-the-move change – the need. As in the manual transmission case (p 94) there are many occasions when it is essential – or certainly useful – to be able to start off in low range, attain a speed where high range can take over and then effect a change of transfer ratios without stopping. The Driver Manual figure of 5 mph will in many cases be too low.

Low/high change – what gear, what speed. The diagram of speed in the gears on p 94, although drawn for the Tdi engine and five-speed manual transmission, reflects a state of affairs similar to that of the four-speed ZF automatic fitted to Discovery and Range Rover. The principle of change-over points remains the same – getting to a high part of the power curve in low range at a speed that will not decay through ground rolling resistance too much to enable transfer to a suitable gear and part of the power curve in the high range.

It is worth learning to obviate the excess torque converter slip that would result from a high load start in high box.

Low-to-high change – procedure. Since the auto transmission will take care of selecting the appropriate main gearbox ratio, it is only necessary (unlike manual p 95) for the driver to attend to the moving of the transfer lever (diagram facing page):

1. Start off in low range with '**3**' selected. Accelerate to 3000 rpm once the gearbox has changed up to 3rd ratio.

2. When at 3000 rpm, simultaneously lift off the throttle and, as the transmission goes from drive to over-run, move the transfer lever aft into neutral.

3. When the rpm have dropped to 1500, ease the transfer lever further aft into the HIGH range position.

Although this is a very simple operation, it will pay to practise it on road and in undemanding conditions before using it in earnest. As with the manual transmission case, it its important to judge movement of the transfer lever into neutral properly.

1.

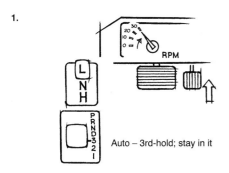

Auto – 3rd-hold; stay in it

2.

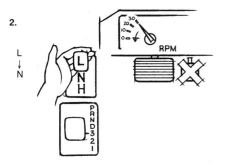

Low to high, mobile. Snick transfer lever into N – remember detent is very small – allow revs to drop, then pull back into H. See text and diagram left.

3.

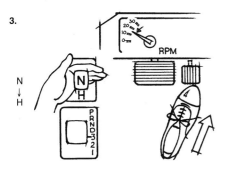

Low to high range on the move. Diagram shows sequence corresponding to text on facing page.

High to low on the move? Sometimes.
Unlike the firm 'No' given on p 95 in the manual case, following the Driver Manual procedure of changing down to low transfer on the move can be done if forward speed is at or under 8 kph (5 mph). Whilst rate of speed decay in worsening conditions will be the same as in the manual case, the auto transmission's ability to re-select the main gear ratio

virtually instantaneously will make this a practical manipulation in cases where speed decay is not too rapid:

1. Slow to 8 kph (5 mph) in HIGH.

2. Lift off accelerator, move main selector to '**N**' and transfer lever to LOW.

3. Re-select '**D**' and drive on.

Unlike manual transmission, high to low with auto can be a useful technique in certain cases.

Land Rover Experience

ENGINE BRAKING

Slippery slopes

Engine braking recommended...but.
Engine braking is the safe way to reduce speed. On long hills use engine braking to keep your speed from building up because that way you are not overheating the brakes – important, since even today's disc brakes can suffer from a degree of 'fade' (reduced efficiency) when they get very hot. All this is a well accepted part of our armoury of safe driving techniques.

Engine braking in general is a safe, economic way of reducing speed.

Sensitive, delicate braking. But think first of a two-wheel drive car on an icy road. Engine braking derives retardation through one pair of wheels on the driven axle whilst sensitive and delicate use of the foot brake uses all four. The same retardation spread between four wheels instead of two reduces the risk of wheel locking. The relevance of this example is to make the point that there is a place for sensitive and delicate braking in many situations in which we have 'learned' to leave the brakes alone. ABS and cadence braking (see Section 3, 'Gentle right foot', p 28) are especially relevant here.

Just as excessive braking can cause wheel slide, so can excessive engine braking – 1st gear low range on a very steep, long, slippery slope.

Beware sliding wheels. In the case of a 4x4 the situation is improved since both engine braking and slowing with the brakes is achieved using all four wheels. But just as excessive use of the brakes can cause lock-up and discontinuity of rolling contact between the wheels and the ground, so excessive engine braking can cause exactly the same thing – sliding wheels. So tackling a really steep slippery slope using 1st gear low box can amount, very occasionally, to excessive engine braking and result in wheel slide. Be ready to use the accelerator. Or it will likely be better to use a higher gear such as 2nd – even 3rd sometimes. (See p 52 and photo top right opposite.)

Be ready to use the accelerator – and keep cadence braking in the back of your mind all the time.

Emergency sequence

Steep initial section, you find you have too low a gear; wheels are sliding.

Emergency procedures

Discs for delicacy. The brakes on all current Land Rover models are power assisted discs, light and sensitively progressive. Delicacy of control is easy to achieve and there are *some* extreme down-slopes where, if you are not equipped with ABS, this delicacy combined with cadence braking (see p 28) will give more controllable retardation than engine braking alone. There are two classic cases to consider:

1. Almost the right gear, brake assistance. Take the case of an initially steep, long slippery down-slope with a loose surface. You judge that 2nd low is appropriate and begin your descent. But the initial section is so steep that the vehicle gains speed faster than you anticipated. Clearly it is inadvisable to attempt to change down at this critical stage (even an automatic will not always change down to 1st in these conditions – see pp 96-99) so a gentle and intermittent use of the brake pedal – gentle cadence braking – can be used to slow the vehicle within the limits of the available grip for the initial steep part of the descent. Do not let the wheels lock; and if they do, release the brakes altogether, immediately.

2. Wrong gear, cadence braking take-over. Take the same steep, long, slippery down-slope. Starting down it in 1st gear low box may result in wheel slide because in such a

Add throttle. Delicate application of brake; quit at the first suspicion of lock-up.

If, in gear, wheels just cannot keep up with speed increase, de-clutch and use cadence braking. Keep front wheels pointing straight down slope.

Select a higher gear once the problem is over, boost the revs as you engage clutch and resume engine braking.

A matter of judgement (above). If it is this steep you want retardation but too low a gear when it is slippery or loose will give you slide. 2nd low, rather than 1st, would be best if it were muddy earth. In the special case of this giant sand dune you need to go higher still – 3rd or 4th low or even 1st high range – to prevent the vehicle nosing into the sand. (In this context see also Glossary 'Castor angle', p 148 and 'Steering feel', p 157.) With ABS (left) the brakes are always a reliable fall-back.

low gear – even with the engine revving hard – the wheels will not be able to turn fast enough to maintain rolling contact with the ground. You realise too late that you have got the wrong gear so, after using all the throttle you can, you must undertake a rescue operation. De-clutch so that the wheels can regain rolling contact with the ground, then with great sensitivity carry out cadence braking – *rapid gentle jabs at the brake pedal that never permit the wheels to lock* but which give you the best

retardation the circumstances allow. The Range Rover's ABS brakes, of course, being anti-lock will carry this operation out for you if you just keep your foot on the clutch and brake pedals; it will signal the fact that ABS is operating by the audible pulses of the brake relay. (While you have the clutch down put the gear lever into 2nd or 3rd ready for when you wish to engage the engine again.) This is a rare scenario but keep it in the back of your mind rather than slide out of control, throttle wide, in 1st.

Emergency procedure: really sensitive use of the brakes, releasing them the instant they lock the wheels – or cadence braking.

TOWING OFF-ROAD

High-density industrial plant trailers (right) need treating with more than expected care off-road – mainly due to inertia and limitations of trailer suspension. Treatment of horse-boxes, boats and the like is more self evident (below).

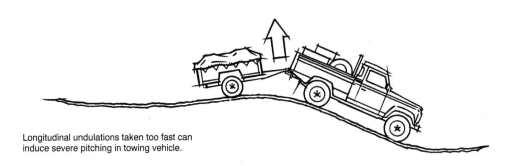

Longitudinal undulations taken too fast can induce severe pitching in towing vehicle.

Potential problems

Heavy trailer off-road – or light trailer driven briskly – will feed back considerable inertia loads to tug.

Greater trailer feedback. (Read Section 4, 'Towing – on-road', p 38 first, noting maximum off-road towing weights shown in the table.) Using trailers off road requires anticipation and care. Feedback effect to the towing vehicle is much more noticeable than on hard road. For example, traversing undulations too fast can cause interactive responses between vehicle and trailer. Specifically, the trailer can cause

considerable pitch in the towing vehicle as it swoops into and out of a dip. This can be bad enough in extreme cases to lift the rear end of the vehicle momentarily off the ground.

Drag, push and lateral roll. Trailer drag over uneven ground and 'trailer-push' down steep slopes will be more pronounced – with braking correspondingly more difficult and liable, in extreme cases, to provoke the trailer to

Land Rover Experience

try and overtake the vehicle in a form of jack-knifing. Off-road there is also a surprising susceptibility to lateral roll. Trailer suspension is seldom damped sufficiently in the laden condition compared to that of the towing vehicle.

Lateral roll over an uneven track which the Land Rover suspension will cope with easily can result in alarming roll angles on the trailer – sometimes resulting in capsizing. (See following pages regarding revolving tow-hooks.)

Beware especially of under-damped lateral roll of trailer on poor tracks.

Trailer influence especially noticeable on steep slippery down-slopes – adversely affected rear wheel adhesion and tendency to jack-knife. Accelerate out of it.

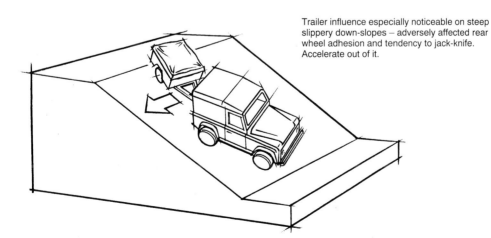

...continued

Towing – off-road – continued

Trailers can avoid an overload situation in expeditions – but tyres must be large and there must be manpower to man-handle the trailer when stuck.

Checks and procedures

Overload solution: provisos. For overlanding expeditions, use of a really robust trailer can be quite an elegant solution to the problem of having a payload requirement in excess of that shown as the maximum for your vehicle on its own. Spreading the load over six wheels is better than the unacceptable alternative of overloading the vehicle's four. The prolonged stress of an overland trip is perhaps an extreme case but it encapsulates the potential problems of all off-road towing so is worth examining.

Keep trailer payload as low as possible to permit low tyre pressures and give combination the best chance off-road.

Four provisos should be remembered for sustained off-road trailer operation:

1. Weight. Minimise the weight of the trailer and load to give the vehicle the best working conditions off-road. An ex-military 750 kg trailer with overrun brakes, loaded to no more than 500 kg gross provides a sensible margin of strength and is in roughly the right category for a Land Rover towing vehicle.

2. Tyres. The same rationale mentioned earlier (see Section 1) about big wheels applies to trailers and is arguably even more important since the trailer wheels are following in ground already cut up by the towing vehicle. Trailer axle load indicated above will enable trailer tyre pressures to be lower than those of the tug and this will enhance flotation in the wake of the towing vehicle. A good rule-of-thumb is to use the same wheels and tyres on the trailer as you have fitted to the towing vehicle. This makes sense functionally, ensures trailer pressures can be lower for best flotation (see Section 7, 'Tyres', p 108) and has the additional advantage that the same spare wheel will fit trailer and towing vehicle.

3. Personnel. There will be times, off road and overlanding, when the trailer has to be detached and man-handled. It will be necessary to have at least two people to do this; three or four will be better still.

4. Towing hitch. The standard 50 mm ball hitch is widely used in the UK and Europe but it should be remembered it is suitable for a maximum gross trailer weight of 1000 kg off-road on all Land Rover products. The European specification ball hitch (Part no RTC9565) is stronger than the standard UK item. Note also the ratings of the 2-bolt and 4-bolt Land Rover Parts combined ball/pin hitches shown on p 38. Because of problems of trailer lateral stability in extreme off-road conditions as noted on p 103, be sure your trailer has an EC-standard hitch that can rotate at the trailer since a tipped trailer would not then affect the towing vehicle.

Pay meticulous attention to condition of towing hitch, bolts and attachment areas.

Example of trailer tyres being larger than those of towing vehicle and thus able to run on lower pressures; better flotation, less drag. Beware, however, since low trailer tyre pressures can cause weaving at speed. Fore and aft motion of loose fitting towing eye over long off-road distance caused considerable wear.

Low range start. As with heavy trailers on hard roads (see Section 4, p 38) there will be many occasions off-road when it will make for a smoother start to move off in low range 2nd gear, continue up the low ratio gears and change into high range on the move using the techniques outlined on pp 94, 96 . For off-road towing, low range is sometimes the better choice to stay in.

Starting in low range with an on-the-move change to high ratio is particularly useful with trailers off-road.

SECTION 7

DATA

TYRES

Tyres function optimally – ie at their very best – in only one set of conditions. Operators can maximise effectiveness – including COST-effectiveness – by careful choice of tyre type, tread type, pressures and driving technique.

Tyre types, axle loads

Tyre types – specialisation vs compromise. For optimum traction there is a specialist tyre for just about every type of terrain. The converse, of course, is also true: whatever tyres you have fitted will have disadvantages on ground other than that for which they were designed. This is a simple fact of life – and the laws of physics – and any attempt to produce a multi-purpose, compromise tyre results in exactly that; a compromise. So, for example, a good mud tyre will be noisy, have a reduced tread life and be not very grippy on tarmac in comparison with a

Specialist tyres exist for every use. The converse of that is that for any variation in vehicle use all tyres are a compromise.

road-optimised tyre which in turn would have poor traction in muddy conditions. In very general terms, most 4x4s spend more time on public roads with tarmac surfaces than they do off-road, however important or challenging their off road forays may be. Thus, in the same general terms, it is sensible to use tyres that do not sacrifice too much of the hard-road grip required for steering and braking. All Land Rover products are supplied with original equipment (OE) tyres appropriate to the needs of *average* model users. The information that follows gives a guide to the strengths and weaknesses of each tyre type.

Land Rover Experience

Tyre types and characteristics		
Road oriented	Optimised for tarmac. Close tread, relatively smooth with sipes ('knife cuts')	**For:** Long life, quiet smooth running, best braking. **Against:** Close tread susceptible to filling in mud, reducing traction.
M+S tyre	M+S = Mud and Snow. Bolder tread version of road tyre. Quite a close, small bold tread. Sometimes provision for studs also.	**For:** As above but slightly less so. Good grip in snow and on grass. **Against:** Better in snow than mud. Close tread susceptible to filling in mud, reducing traction. (Note: Tread too bold to give good performance on dry sand.)
Mud tyre	Big, bold, open tread pattern with sharp right-angle edges	**For:** Very good in all types of mud. **Against:** Grip on wet tarmac slightly impaired. 'Heel and toe' wear on tread blocks shortens life. Noisy. (Note: Poor on dry sand.)
Multi purpose	Combination of mud tyre and road tyre build – usually a zig-zag centre band with bold transverse edge lugs.	**For:** A good compromise for frequent on/off road use, eg farming. **Against:** Grip on wet tarmac slightly impaired on some multi-purpose tyres. Wears faster than road tyre, slightly noisy. (Note: Poor on dry sand.)
Sand tyres	Subtly shaped tread with shouldered blocks to compress sand in 'cups' (enhancing flotation and traction) rather than cut through it.	**For:** Very good for extracting last gramme of traction from sand. Robust enough for all desert terrain. **Against:** Poorer grip on wet tarmac must be allowed for. Some 'heel and toe' wear on tread blocks, some noise. (Note: Good flotation but poor performance in mud.)
Tyres for rock	There are no tyres made specially for rock – by rock is meant any rough surface of large or small angular rocks or stones. The key to traversing rock lies with the driver – see Section 4, p 64. Clearly a robust tyre is best, in most cases a radial with a reinforced tread – but see below. The M+S, mud and multi-purpose types listed above would do well though the mud and multi-purpose tyres would have greater tread thickness – but see below for special conditions applicable to sustained off-road operations in rocky conditions without on-road use*.	

*Cross-ply tyres. Where operations are almost exclusively off-road on rock or stone – such as fleet operations in quarries – the more damage-resistant qualities (at full inflation pressures) of cross-ply tyres could help keep operating costs down. It is essential, however, to consider and accommodate the following criteria:

a. Virtually all 7.50 x 16 cross-plies are – see table p 117 – 'L' speed rated, ie limited to 120 kph(75 mph), so should not be fitted to high powered vehicles operating on-road.

b. Cross-ply tyres have higher rolling resistance so will marginally reduce fuel economy.

c. Cross-plies have marginally less grip than radials on-road so handling affected.

Tyre designers have an impossible task trying to cater for all uses. Learn as much as you can about tyres and you will enormously enhance their effectiveness.

...continued

Tyres – continued

If a fleet operator seldom runs his vehicles on road or at GVW, weighing representative vehicles to determine typical axle loads could establish an acceptably lower tyre pressure that would enhance off-road performance fleet-wide.

Tyre pressures and axle loads are interdependent – both affect sidewall deflection, a critical criterion.

Tyre pressures – relevance of axle loads.
Tyres give their optimum performance – the best combination of grip, handling response, operating temperature (important for structural reasons) and a degree of shock absorbtion – when their elements (tread, beads and sidewalls) are optimally disposed to one another. The main criterion in determining this is sidewall deflection and this is established by the load on the tyre and its internal pressure. There is thus a theoretically optimum tyre pressure for every change in axle load or payload within the vehicle; this is why front and rear tyre pressures are different. In practice (and to ensure you do not spend your whole life changing tyre

pressures) there is some latitude and usually two sets (ie front and rear) of pressures are quoted for vehicles – one for the unladen and one for the fully laden condition. These, of course, are based on individual front and rear axle loads – the weight each axle carries. Because they will be of use in determining the pressures to be used with specialist tyres – ie any not shown on the following pages – a table of axle loads for all Land Rover vehicles is given on the facing page.

Actual axle loads – front and rear					
Vehicle type Maximum weights GVW and maximum individual axle loads. See notes 1 and 2. GVW/front/rear max	Body type and/or manual/auto	Axle loads at kerb weight – 2.5 petrol engine Front/rear Kg	Axle loads at kerb weight – V8 petrol engine Front/rear Kg	Axle loads at kerb weight – 2.5D or VM engine Front/rear Kg	Axle loads at kerb weight – Tdi engine Front/rear Kg
Defender 90 Std: 2400/1200/1380 Hi-load suspension: 2550/1200/1500	Soft top Pick up Hard top Station wagon	922/714 919/717 916/767 911/790	908/719 905/722 902/770 897/793	946/710 943/722 940/763 935/786	971/724 967/727 960/786 959/834
Defender 110 Levelled suspension: 2950/1200/1750 Unlevelled susp'n: 3050/1200/1850	Soft top Pick up Hi cap pick up Hard top Station wagon County	941/864 940/875 938/915 938/902 924/1019 935/1044	941/865 939/876 937/916 937/903 935/1009 935/1045	972/856 972/867 970/907 970/897 955/1014 966/1039	1004/868 1000/880 998/919 994/919 982/1036 993/1061
Defender 130 3500/1500/2200	Crew cab HCPU	-	1027/985	-	1070/1016
Discovery V8: 2720/1100/1650 Tdi: 2720/1200/1650	3 dr manual 3 dr auto 5 dr manual 5 dr auto	- - - -	921/998 921/998 921/1065 921/1065	- - - -	991/1017 - 1006/1047 -
Range Rover 3.9 V8: 2510/1100/1510 Tdi Diesel: 2510/1200/1510 4.2 LSE: 2620/1200/1620	2 dr manual 2 dr auto 4 dr manual 4 dr auto LSE	- - - - -	952/968 979/972 964/922 980/1020 1070/1080	1027/1004 - 1039/1027 - -	1024/1028 - 1024/1028 - -

NOTE 1: Gross vehicle weight (GVW), ie weight fully laden, is the maximum weight for which the suspension was designed so is constant for a given vehicle type. Only where the suspension itself has an alternative specification, as in the Defender 90 and Defender 110, or where heavier diesel engines are fitted, are different GVWs or GVW axle loads shown.

NOTE 2: Because it is not always easy to get weight distribution front/rear precisely correct, individual axles may be loaded to the 'max' figures shown so long as the *overall* GVW is not exceeded. Note that in most cases the sum of the front and rear 'max' figures would exceed the GVW so do not load both axles to max. The Defender 110 has max and actual axle loads at GVW that are the same.

NOTE 3: Kerb weight, sometimes called 'EEC kerb', is defined as unladen weight plus full fuel plus a 75 kg driver.

Do axle loads really matter? In a word, yes. The reason you are reading this section at all is that you want *the best* flotation and performance from your tyres under specific conditions; clearly you do not want this if it will hazard your vehicles' safety or durability or damage your tyres. Applying the correct axle loads – accurate to within 100 kg will do – to tyre data from a manufacturer will enable you to select a pressure that will yield best flotation and performance without compromising safety

and durability. The span of the figures is considerable; an unladen Defender 90 rear axle carries only 38% of the load that the rear axle of laden Defender 110. That matters. The above table can be used to interpolate axle loads – between unladen and fully laden – for your particular type of operations. For precise further details contact the tyre manufacturer but they will need the axle loads given above. Axle load is greatly (and surprisingly) affected by load distribution – see diagrams on p 123.

If you want the best tyre performance or want to save the time wasted in recovery in your fleet, check axle loads and tyre pressures.

...continued

Tyres – continued

Optimum pressures

Tyre pressures – three conditions. To get the best out of your tyres and vehicle on roads, on tracks and poor roads and in emergency flotation conditions you need three sets of tyre pressures. As we have seen (pp 12, 56–59, 113 opposite) lowering tyre pressures increases the size of the tyre 'footprint' and thus lowers the unit pressure on the ground. The ground is thus less stressed and will yield better traction and flotation, so assisting a vehicle in traversing difficult terrain or in self-recovery if it is stuck. But we have also seen that a tyre has an optimum operating pressure. This assumes given criteria of handling response and maximum speed.

Limit the speed. It follows, therefore, that if we reduce the tyre pressures we must also accept different handling characteristics and, for structural and safety reasons, also *limit the maximum speed when at reduced pressures.* The tables that follow list (at kerb weight and at maximum permitted laden weight), firstly, normal road pressures which assume best

handling and unlimited speed; secondly, 'tracks and poor road' pressures which might be applicable to tracks with more difficult off-road diversions; and finally 'emergency flotation' is listed where the terrain requires the absolute maximum flotation and traction. This latter would be applicable to terrain at the limits of your vehicle's off-road capabilities or for self-recovery from a bogged situation; such use *must be followed by re-inflation to appropriate road or tracks pressures.*

Preliminary note: For reasons of simplicity of operation, Land Rover handbooks quote a single set of front / rear tyre pressures (shown underlined in the tables here) catering for all conditions up to maximum load on hard roads. However, where flotation, traction and / or comfort are important, operators should follow the lower pressure recommendations in the tables on this and the next spread. (Note that these pressures assume 'normal' ambient temperatures – about 15°C ±10°. Tyre pressure should *always* be checked 'cold', ie after the vehicle has been standing for an hour or more; never 'bleed' pressure from a warmed-up tyre. If ambient temperatures are high – around 30–45°C – increase all inflation pressures shown by 10% – eg 2.0 bar would be 2.2.)

Different tyre pressures for different conditions. ESSENTIAL to keep within speed and load limitations and reinflate tyres when back on easier ground.

Defender 90 – tyre pressure in bars (bars to psi – see table p 117)						
Tyre no	Tyre name and size	Load index / speed symbol (See p 117)	Vehicle weight	Hard-road pressures (to max speed)	Tracks and poor roads. 40 mph max	Off-road emergency flotation 12 mph max
				Front / rear	Front / rear	Front / rear
1.	Michelin 205 R 16 X M+S	99Q	Kerb GVW	1.9 / 2.1 <u>1.9 / 2.4</u>	1.6 / 1.9 1.7 / 2.1	1.2 / 1.2 1.2 / 1.4
2.	Michelin 7.50 R 16 X 4x4 Michelin 7.50 R 16 X-CL Michelin 7.50 R 16 XS	108N 112L 108N	Kerb GVW	1.8 / 2.0 <u>1.9 / 2.9</u>	1.4 / 1.6 1.5 / 2.2	1.1 / 1.2 1.1 / 1.7
3.	Goodyear 7.50 R 16 G90	108N	Kerb GVW	1.8 / 2.0 <u>1.9 / 2.9</u>	1.4 /1.6 1.5 / 2.2	1.1 / 1.2 1.1 / 1.7
				NB: Single, all-loads pressure underlined		

Defender 110 – tyre pressure in bars (bars to psi – see table p 117)						
Tyre no	Tyre name and size	Load index / speed symbol (See p 117)	Vehicle weight	Hard-road pressures (to max speed)	Tracks and poor roads. 40 mph max	Off-road emergency flotation 12 mph max
				Front / rear	Front / rear	Front / rear
1.	Michelin 7.50 R16 X 4x4 Michelin 7.50 R16 X-CL Michelin 7.50 R16 XS Michelin 7.50 R16 X ZY	108N 112L 108N 112L	Kerb GVW	1.8 / 2.0 1.9 / 3.3	1.4 / 1.6 1.5 / 2.5	1.1 / 1.2 1.1 / 2.0
2.	Avon Rangemaster 7.50 R16	108/106N	Kerb GVW	1.8 / 2.1 1.9 / 3.3	1.6 / 1.6 1.8 / 2.1	1.1 / 1.1 1.1 / 1.8
3.	Goodyear 7.50 R 16 G90	108N	Kerb GVW	1.8 /2.1 1.9 /3.3	1.4 /1.6 1.5 / 2.5	1.1 / 1.2 1.1 / 2.0
				NB: Single, all-loads pressure underlined		

Tyre footprint of Michelin XS at (left to right) road pressures, track pressure and emergency flotation pressure. Percentage increases in area are considerable.

Details count - even when you are having a difficult time. Always use tyre valve caps and replace them - without dirt and grit on the inside – when deflating and re-inflating tyres

Defender 130 – tyre pressure in bars (bars to psi – see table p 117)						
Tyre no	Tyre name and size	Load index / speed symbol (See p 117)	Vehicle weight	Hard-road pressures (to max speed)	Tracks and poor roads. 40 mph max	Off-road emergency flotation 12 mph max
				Front / rear	Front / rear	Front / rear
1.	Michelin 7.50 R16 X 4x4 Michelin 7.50 R16 X-CL Michelin 7.50 R16 XS Michelin 750 R16 X ZY	108N 112L 108N 112L	Kerb GVW	1.9 / 2.1 3.0 / 4.5	1.6 / 1.6 2.4 / 3.6	1.2 / 1.3 1.8 / 2.8
				NB: Single, all-loads pressure underlined		

...continued

Land Rover Experience

Tyres – continued

\multicolumn{7}{c}{**Discovery – tyre pressure in bars (bars to psi – see table p 117)**}
Tyre no	Tyre name and size	Load index/ speed symbol (see p 117)	Vehicle weight	Hard road pressures (to max speed) _Front/rear_	Tracks and poor roads 40 mph max _Front/rear_	Off-road emergency flotation 12 mph max _Front/rear_
1.	Michelin 205 R 16 XM+S 244 TL	104T	Kerb GVW	1.9 / 2.2 1.9 / 2.6	1.6 / 2.0 1.6 / 2.3	1.2 / 1.2 1.2 / 1.4
2.	Michelin 235/70 R 16 4x4 TL	105H	Kerb GVW	1.8 / 2.0 1.8 / 2.3	1.6 / 1.8 1.6 / 2.0	1.2 / 1.2 1.2 / 1.4
3.	Pirelli Akros 205 R 16	104S	Kerb GVW	1.6 / 1.8 1.9 / 2.6	1.3 / 1.4 1.6 / 2.2	1.1 / 1.2 1.4 / 1.9
4.	Goodyear Wrangler 205 R 16	104T	Kerb GVW	1.9 / 2.2 1.9 /2.6	1.6 / 2.0 1.6 / 2.3	1.2 / 1.2 1.2 / 1.4

NB: Single, all-loads pressure underlined

Make it easy if you can. Re-inflation by muscle power is very hard work taking four tyres from emergency low to track pressures – especially in hot climates. Small cheap electric pumps (photo opposite) are effective but get hot. It is worth having two – one cooling while the other is pumping. Where there is a repeated heavy duty working requirement for re-inflation, using a line from the air brakes compressor (where fitted, see p 41) or from a unit such as the ARB (left) fitted to one vehicle amongst a team may be more suitable. The ARB is actually designed for a locking axle differential but can inflate tyres as well.

\multicolumn{7}{c}{**Range Rover – tyre pressure in bars (bars to psi – see table p 117)**}
Tyre no	Tyre name and size	Load index / speed symbol (See p 117)	Vehicle weight	Hard-road pressures (to max speed) _Front / rear_	Tracks and poor roads 40 mph max _Front / rear_	Off-road emergency flotation 12 mph max _Front / rear_
1.	Michelin 205 R 16 XM+S 244 TL	104T	Kerb GVW	1.9 / 2.1 1.9 / 2.4	1.6 / 1.9 1.6 / 2.1	1.2 / 1.2 1.2 / 1.4
2.	Goodyear Wrangler 205 R16	104T	Kerb GVW	1.9 / 2.1 1.9 / 2.4	1.6 / 1.9 1.6 / 2.1	1.2 / 1.2 1.2/ 1.4

NB: Single, all-loads pressure underlined

Land Rover Experience

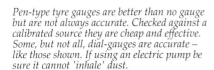

Pen-type tyre gauges are better than no gauge but are not always accurate. Checked against a calibrated source they are cheap and effective. Some, but not all, dial-gauges are accurate – like those shown. If using an electric pump be sure it cannot 'inhale' dust.

Tyre pressures – speed warning. It is important to emphasise the speed limitations at reduced pressures shown in the columns above. *Never exceed the speed limits shown here.* Driving too fast on under-inflated tyres will cause structural damage to your tyres through over-heating and possible de-lamination of the carcass; it will usually produce unacceptable handling and the possibility of rolling the tyres off the rims on corners. Be sure always to be equipped with an accurate tyre pressure gauge and a re-inflation pump if you are going off roading.

Pressure gauges, re-inflation. It has often been shown that concern for and care of tyres can be set at naught by that weakest of weak links the tyre pressure gauge. The pen-type gauge is often inaccurate and some dial gauges are not necessarily an improvement. Others, however, are good but should still be checked against one or more air hoses at service stations. In the UK such hoses and gauges have to be checked by law and can usually be relied upon. Once you have your accurate, proven tyre gauge, keep it in a dust-proof plastic bag in the vehicle at all times. Re-inflation of the tyres after pressure reduction for-off road work is best done by

an electric pump carried with you. Again you should be circumspect about the standard of unit you buy. Tyres fitted to Land Rover vehicles need a lot of air compared to car tyres so get a pump that is large, robust and can stand up to long periods of use without overheating.

Tubeless tyres. When severe off-road conditions are likely it is in most cases sensible, for two reasons, to fit tubes in your tyres. Firstly, encountering extreme conditions of roughness when inflation has been reduced to emergency soft could conceivably cause unseating of a tubeless tyre from the rim and thus cause total loss of pressure. Secondly, severe off-road conditions are often associated with operations away from full service facilities. Whilst changing or repairing a tyre by hand in the field is possible with a tubed tyre, the same thing would not be possible with a tubeless tyre. A note, however, about alloy wheels which are designed with an internal AH (asymmetric hump) rim profile to enhance bead retention at very low pressures; these wheels are not recommended for use with tubes since low pressure flexing of the tyre can cause chafing of the tubes on the internal rim humps.

WARNING. A repeated warning about NEVER exceeding the speed and load limitations on tyres at reduced pressures.

Obtain – and take care of – a good and accurate tyre pressure gauge.

...continued

Land Rover Experience

Tyres- continued

Data on load and speed ratings, tyre construction and build are inscribed on the sidewall – see diagram opposite for full data and tables below for de-coding load index and speed symbol. Thus the Michelin X M+S 244 in the photographs, having a 99T load/speed rating is cleared to a maximum load per tyre of 775 kg up to 118 mph (at appropriate pressures).

If you have to buy an unfamiliar tyre, everything you need to know about it will be written on the sidewall. If it isn't, don't buy it.

Tyre nomenclature. A considerable amount of information is inscribed on the sidewall (and tread) of tyres, all of which is relevant to its specification – despite the assurances of those who would try to sell you tyres that are 'the same' as the one you specifically seek. The principal dimensions of a tyre are its *width* – not the depth between tread and bead – and the wheel diameter to which it is fitted. Thus a '7.50 x 16' is a tyre designed for a 16 inch diameter wheel and having a normal inflated width – ie the external maximum width of the inflated, unladen tyre – of 7.50 inches; it is not necessarily the width of the tread itself. This width data can also be shown in millimetres (still allied to a rim size in inches) as in the 205 x 16. Other criteria, some of which are shown in the diagram opposite, are:

Manufacturer's generic name such as 'X'
Manufacturer's type number or name, eg XCL, Rangemaster, Wrangler
Metric width in mm, eg 205, 235
Aspect ratio (cross section height:width ratio percentage)
      - follows metric width when shown (would be 235/70).
'R' for radial
Overall tyre diameter (usually given in the US)
Load index/speed symbol – see tables opposite
Maximum load and pressure – in lb and psi in addition to load index (US requirement)
Sidewall and tread construction – plies and material, eg steel, rayon (US requirement)
Ply rating – (equivalent) sidewall plies in a crossply tyre
Wear indicators
Country of manufacture
Direction of rotation – sometimes shown
ECE and US Dept of Transport type approval mark

Tyre sidewall markings

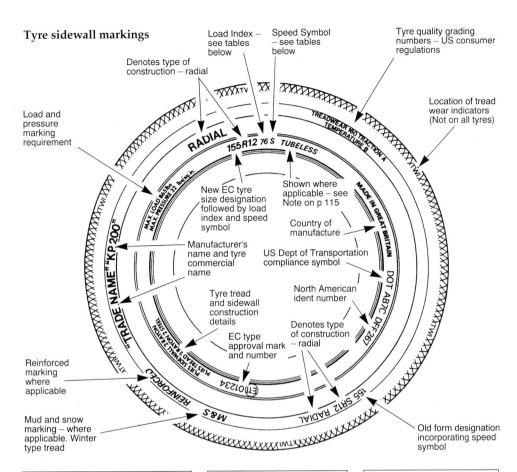

Tyre Load Index			
(NB Max load <u>per-tyre</u> at full road pressures at speed shown by accompanying speed symbol)			
Index	kg	Index	kg
97	730	111	1090
98	750	112	1120
99	775	113	1150
100	800	114	1180
101	825	115	1215
102	850	116	1250
103	875	117	1285
104	900	118	1320
105	925	119	1360
106	950	120	1400
107	975	121	1450
108	1000	122	1500
109	1030	123	1550
110	1060	124	1600

Tyre Speed Symbol		
(NB Max speed at full road pressures at per-tyre load shown by load index)		
Symbol	kph	mph
J	100	62
K	110	68
L	120	75
M	130	81
N	140	87
P	150	95
Q	160	100
R	170	105
S	180	113
T	190	118
U	200	125
H	210	130
V	240	150
VR	210/240	130/150

Tyre pressures – bars to (nearest whole) psi			
Bars	psi	Bars	psi
1.1	16	2.7	39
1.2	17	2.8	41
1.3	19	2.9	42
1.4	20	3.0	44
1.5	22	3.1	45
1.6	23	3.2	46
1.7	25	3.3	48
1.8	26	3.4	49
1.9	27	3.5	51
2.0	29	3.6	52
2.1	30		
2.2	32	4.3	62
2.3	33	4.4	64
2.4	35	4.5	65
2.5	36	4.6	67
2.6	38	4.7	68

LOADING

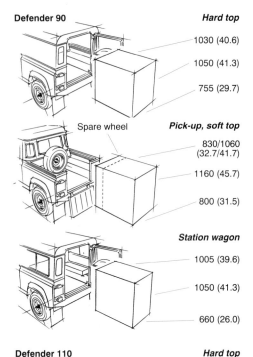

Defender 90

Hard top

1030 (40.6)

1050 (41.3)

755 (29.7)

Spare wheel

Pick-up, soft top

830/1060 (32.7/41.7)

1160 (45.7)

800 (31.5)

Station wagon

1005 (39.6)

1050 (41.3)

660 (26.0)

Defender 110

Hard top

1750 (68.9)

1050 (41.3)

755 (29.7)

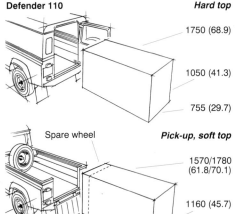

Spare wheel

Pick-up, soft top

1570/1780 (61.8/70.1)

1160 (45.7)

800 (31.5)

Station wagon

1100/1470 (43.3/57.9)

1050 (41.4)

660 (26.0)

Seats rolled forward

Capacity – weight and bulk

Margins of durability, strength, handling and braking will be eroded if you overload.

Never overload. This is probably the prime rule in operating any vehicle and, despite their reputation for strength, it applies to Land Rover products as well. *Every* engineered object has strength criteria to which it is designed – with margins that are adequate or generous according to design philosophy. To overload is to eat into strength and durability margins and, in the case of cargo in vehicles, will adversely affect handling and performance as well. Payloads for your particular vehicle appear in the Technical Data section that follows – pp 126-145.

Minimise off-road weights. For a given duty load choose a vehicle specification which will comfortably cope with the weight involved rather than be on the limits. Do not exceed specification payload and gross vehicle weights (GVW).

Load density – weight vs bulk. A cubic foot of lead vs a cubic foot of compressed straw is an analogy of weight vs bulk that would immediately catch our attention. But in the rough and tumble of day to day fleet operation with loads of less obvious density variation it can be forgotten. This is particularly the case with high density loads where the availability of *space* can often obscure the fact that the payload limit has been reached. Operators should be especially alert to this and – see p 122 – pay attention to load distribution as well.

Remember load density. Just because there is room in the vehicle does not mean you have the spare payload.

approx 15 mm – clear all round)

Defender 110/130 Hi Cap

Defender 110 HCPU

1060 (41.7)

1980 (78.0)

1160 (45.7)

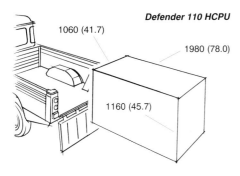

Defender 130 HCPU

1060 (41.7)

1640 (64.6)

1160 (45.7)

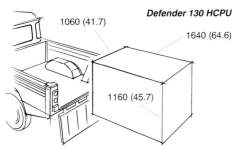

Discovery *3-door, 5-door Rear seats up*

1020 (40.2) 520 (20.5)

1080 (42.5)

Rear seats rolled forward

1020 (40.2)

1080 (42.5)

1220 (48.0)

Range Rover *100, 108 inch wheelbase Rear seats up*

820 (32.3) 530 (20.9)

800 (31.5) 1000 (39.4)

1175 (46.23) LSE: 1275 (50.2) Rear seats rolled forward

820 (32.8)

1000 (39.4)

1415 (55.7) LSE:1515 (59.6)

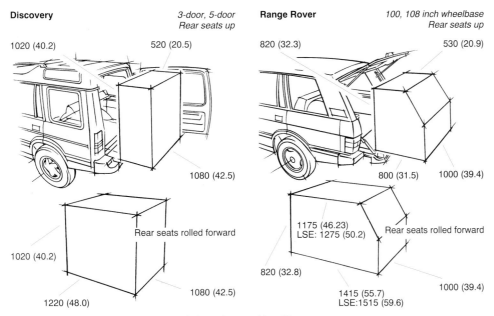

Exact length depends on position of front seats

Loading – continued

Capacity – weight and bulk
contd

Generic payload span*	
Defender 90	654–923 kg
Defender 110	1023–1245 kg
Defender 130	1400 kg +
Discovery	667–801 kg
Range Rover	458–543 kg

*Depending on engine, body type, suspension and transmission. See pp 126–145 for precise payloads for your vehicle.

Typical unit weights	
205 litre (45 Imp gal) barrel, empty	20 kg
205 litre barrel full of petrol, kerosene	185 kg
" " diesel, lube oil	200 kg
" " water	225 kg
20 litre (4.5 Imp gal) steel jerry can, empty	4 kg
20 litre steel jerry can full of petrol, kerosene	20 kg
" " diesel, lube oil	22 kg
" " water	24 kg

Standard 205 litre (45 Imp gal) barrel, jerry can
mm, (inches)

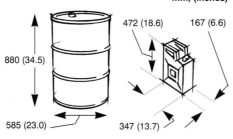

880 (34.5)

585 (23.0)

472 (18.6)   167 (6.6)

347 (13.7)

Tables show payload span of Land Rover product range and can be used with unit weights and diagrams opposite to get a feel for bulk/weight relationship of typical standard-unit loads. Oil drums can be rolled into Hi Cap through its wider tailgate (below, upper photo); they will fit, lying down, between standard Defender wheelboxes but cannot be rolled through tailgate (lower photo).

Bulk and weight – common loads compared

Defender 90/110 – standard pick-ups

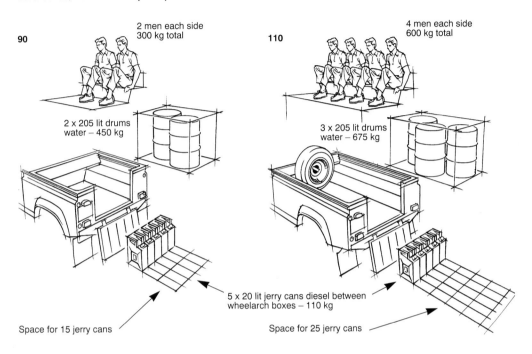

90

2 men each side
300 kg total

110

4 men each side
600 kg total

2 x 205 lit drums
water – 450 kg

3 x 205 lit drums
water – 675 kg

5 x 20 lit jerry cans diesel between
wheelarch boxes – 110 kg

Space for 15 jerry cans

Space for 25 jerry cans

Defender 110/130 – High Capacity pick-ups

110 HCPU: 5 x 205 lit drums diesel – 1000 kg
5 x 205 lit drums water weigh 1125 kg
(*NB Space available for 6 drums but max
payload is 1087 kg*)

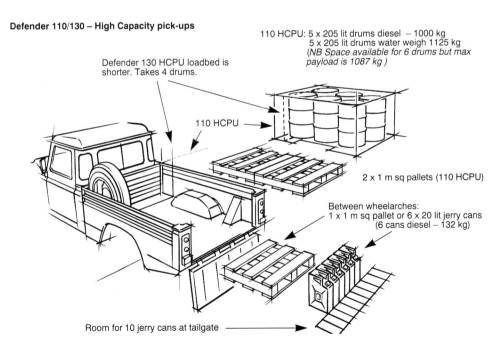

Defender 130 HCPU loadbed is
shorter. Takes 4 drums.

110 HCPU

2 x 1 m sq pallets (110 HCPU)

Between wheelarches:
1 x 1 m sq pallet or 6 x 20 lit jerry cans
(6 cans diesel – 132 kg)

Room for 10 jerry cans at tailgate

Land Rover Experience

Loading – continued

Weight distribution

Weight distribution would be better termed weight concentration. Concentrate it low down and at the front of the load bed.

Normal weight distribution. As the table on p 111 has already shown, all Land Rover products are designed to take a greater load on their springs and axles at the rear when fully laden because that is the inevitable nature of the easy-access bonneted design.

Low down, 50/50 fore and aft. However, a degree of control over weight distribution lies with the operator (or operators' operative). From a handling and flotation point of view in the most demanding conditions, the nearer a vehicle can get to a 50/50 fore and aft axle load condition the better it will be. Except with the lightest loads, even front/rear distribution will not be possible but keeping the main load ahead of the rear axle and as low down as possible will enhance both handling and flotation.

In on-the-limit flotation conditions 50/50 front/rear axle loads will give best chance of getting through.

Excessive roof rack load – above – increases chance of tipping. (Note Camel Trophy vehicles have internal roll-cages which increase roof strength.) Photographs below show Land Rover Parts approved roof racks – ideal for bulky, relatively light, items such as surf-boards, skis or ladders. Maximum recommended roof load is 75 kg (50 kg for Discovery). Internally stowed and lashed loads (see next spread) are preferable to roof racks like that above.

Distribution within the load. Thus even within a given load which may get close to your vehicle's maximum GVW it is sensible to place high density items at the front of the load bed and as close to the floor as possible. A vehicle bogging in soft desert sand or in mud will all too often be seen to sink at the rear first because of less than ideal weight distribution; evening-out the fore and aft load will help.

Check weights for best tyre pressures. Users regularly operating in limiting flotation conditions at less than maximum payload where rear axle load is low, can benefit from a calculated assessment of how low rear tyre pressures can go. Where standard loads or load kits are involved it would pay, as suggested on p 110, to have

Avoid roof rack or anything that will increase vehicle's moment of inertia. If you really do need one, put only light loads on it.

a vehicle weighed front and rear to determine what axle loads really are.

Roof racks, external bolt-ons. A natural corollary of this attention to weight distribution is the elimination, where possible, of roof racks or other external bolt-on paraphenalia. These items increase a vehicle's moment of inertia in pitch and roll and can be a safety hazard when mis-

Variation of axle load with load position – 250 kg load

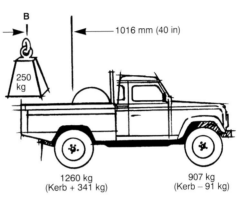

250 kg

610 mm (24 in)

1114 kg
(Kerb + 195 kg)

1052 kg
(Kerb + 55 kg)

Defender 110 HCPU Tdi at kerb weight

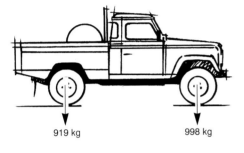

919 kg

998 kg

B

250 kg

1016 mm (40 in)

1260 kg
(Kerb + 341 kg)

907 kg
(Kerb − 91 kg)

NB. *Danger of exceeding axle weights.*
A 638 kg load positioned aft at B would
increase rear axle load to the top limit of
1850 kg. Front axle load in this case
would be 250 kg lighter than at kerb
weight.

*CAUTION. Poorly
distributed load – too
far aft – can result in
rear axle load be
exceeded.*

used. Many expedition Land Rover
vehicles have been grossly overloaded on
the roof rack – and some, unsurprisingly,
have paid the price by tipping. There are
many operators, however, for whom a roof
rack is essential and in these cases
remember that the maximum roof load
recommended for a Defender and Range
Rover is 75 kg (50 kg for Discovery). This
is enough to accommodate light bulky

items such as ladders, small-section timber,
canoes and the like.

Effect of trailers. Remember that a trailer,
with its appropriate trailer preponderance
(see pp 38 and 102), will, for a given actual
nose load, exert a disproportionately high
download on the rear axle because the tow
hitch is well aft of the axle line. This is
another reason for keeping cargo forward.

*Count trailer nose-
weight as payload
and remember its
effect on vehicle
dynamics – see
pp 38, 102.*

...continued

Land Rover Experience

Loading – continued

Lashing cleats – military vehicle shown above – may be fitted to any Land Rover. Part number is RRC 3588/3674 plus locknuts. Older version (left, below) from 1-tonne, is 395104. Typical suitable lashing straps are shown – 1-inch and 1.5-inch webbing with over-centre tensioners.

Securing the load

Rattle-free load carriers get driven well; lash the load.

Eliminating rattles, good driving. A rattling, sliding load jars the nerves as much as it does the vehicle and those who have experienced both will attest the beneficial effects of a well-secured load (and the resultant reduction of noise) on their driving ability and general composure. Noisy, rattling vehicles tend to be driven without consideration and the converse is true – a quiet, rattle-free vehicle is driven smoothly and with mechanical sympathy. The pay-off for this in multi-vehicle fleet operations and also in overland expeditions is notable in terms of reducing the stress the vehicle undergoes in difficult conditions.

Tie-downs. In general, loads may be stabilised by using rope in the cleats around the periphery of the Defender pick-

Load lashing in practice: nowhere is it more important than on overland expeditions of the kind shown here using the Land Rover military One Tonne. Though expedition routine makes load lashing second nature, it need not be a chore in give-and-take fleet operation if thought is given to placing of cleats and provision of straps.

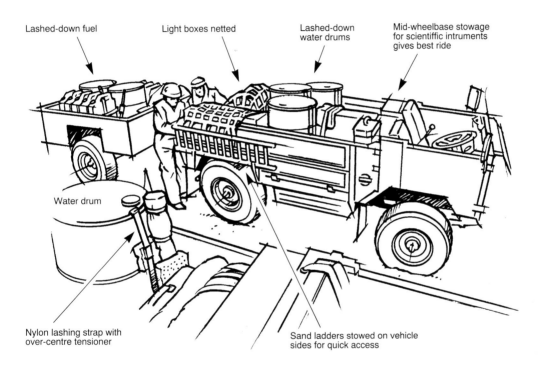

Lashed-down fuel

Light boxes netted

Lashed-down water drums

Mid-wheelbase stowage for scientiffic intruments gives best ride

Water drum

Nylon lashing strap with over-centre tensioner

Sand ladders stowed on vehicle sides for quick access

up cargo area. The ease with which the cargo area of virtually any Land Rover product can be customised with tie-downs makes the securing of planned loads a very straightforward business. Robust-gauge aluminium alloy panels permit tie-down cleats to be bolted into position without the risk of corrosion causing subsequent damage; position them astride strengtheners where possible. Military versions of Defenders have usually got

these cleats in position already but the same parts (RRC 3588/3674) may be obtained from Land Rover dealerships for tailored installations. Use lashing straps with hooks and non-slip tighteners.

Cargo nets. A simple, unfussy way to secure a mixed load, particularly of 'soft' items, is to use a cargo net over a small tarpaulin and roped to the hood-canvas cleats.

Install internal lashing cleats to suit your most-used cargo format and use built-for-purpose lashing straps.

TECHNICAL DATA – DEFENDER 90

Weights

Model	90 Soft Top				90 Pick-Up				90 Hard Top				90 Station Wagon			
Engine	2.5P	3.5P	2.5D	2.5Tdi	2.5P	3.5P	2.5D	2.5Tdi	2.5P	3.5P	2.5D	2.5Tdi	2.5P	3.5P	2.5D	2.5Tdi
Gross vehicle weight kg	Standard suspension: 2400															
Kerb weight kg	1636	1627	1656	1695	1636	1627	1665	1694	1683	1672	1703	1746	1701	1690	1721	1793
Payload kg	764	773	744	705	764	773	735	706	717	728	697	654	699	710	679	607
Gross vehicle weight kg	High load suspension: 2550															
Kerb weight kg	1640	1627	1660	1699	1640	1627	1669	1698	1687	1672	1707	1750	1705	1690	1725	1797
Payload kg	910	923	890	851	910	923	881	852	863	878	843	800	845	860	825	753
Seating capacity	2 – 7				2 – 7				2 – 7				6 – 7			

Defender 90 comes in four body options, each with four engine options, standard or high load suspension, manual or power assisted steering, two tyre-size options.

Exterior dimensions – mm (ins)

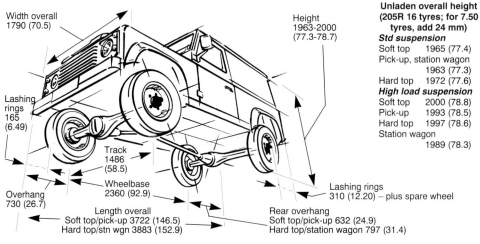

Width overall
1790 (70.5)

Height
1963-2000
(77.3-78.7)

Lashing
rings
165
(6.49)

Track
1486
(58.5)

Wheelbase
2360 (92.9)

Overhang
730 (26.7)

Length overall
Soft top/pick-up 3722 (146.5)
Hard top/stn wgn 3883 (152.9)

Rear overhang
Soft top/pick-up 632 (24.9)
Hard top/station wagon 797 (31.4)

Lashing rings
310 (12.20) – plus spare wheel

Unladen overall height
(205R 16 tyres; for 7.50
tyres, add 24 mm)
Std suspension
Soft top   1965 (77.4)
Pick-up, station wagon
                       1963 (77.3)
Hard top   1972 (77.6)
High load suspension
Soft top   2000 (78.8)
Pick-up   1993 (78.5)
Hard top   1997 (78.6)
Station wagon
                       1989 (78.3)

Wheelbase is 92.9 inches – the '90' name is wheelbase rounded to nearest 10 inches.

Interior dimensions – mm (ins)

See also p 118 – biggest slide-in box

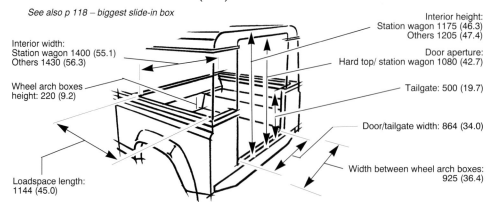

Interior width:
Station wagon 1400 (55.1)
Others 1430 (56.3)

Wheel arch boxes
height: 220 (9.2)

Loadspace length:
1144 (45.0)

Interior height:
Station wagon 1175 (46.3)
Others 1205 (47.4)

Door aperture:
Hard top/ station wagon 1080 (42.7)

Tailgate: 500 (19.7)

Door/tailgate width: 864 (34.0)

Width between wheel arch boxes:
925 (36.4)

Length of load space times interior width gives load area of 1.63 sq metres.

Geometric limitations

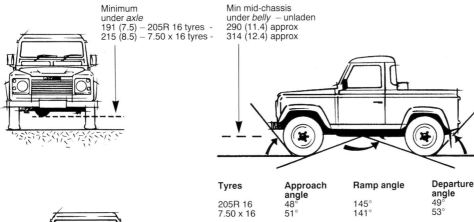

Minimum
under *axle*
191 (7.5) – 205R 16 tyres -
215 (8.5) – 7.50 x 16 tyres -

Min mid-chassis
under *belly* – unladen
290 (11.4) approx
314 (12.4) approx

Tyres	Approach angle	Ramp angle	Departure angle
205R 16	48°	145°	49°
7.50 x 16	51°	141°	53°

Normal wading
depth 500 (19.7).
See p 68 re wading
plugs

*Max payloads of
654-923 kg give
cargo 90s best
power to weight
ratio of the
Defenders; best
articulation of
product range gives
best off-road
potential.*

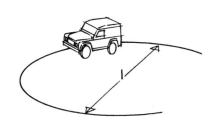

Minimum kerb-kerb turning circle:
205R 16 tyres 11.7 m (38.4 ft)
7.50 x 16 tyres 12.3 m (40.4 ft)
6.00 x 16 tyres 11.5 m (37.7 ft)

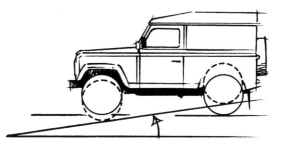

Longitudinal articulation coefficient (see Glossary p 154)
C_{LA}= 17.14

*Beam axles and coil
springs front and
rear. Disc brakes
front, drums rear,
servo assisted. Power
assisted steering
standard. (UK)*

CHASSIS
Type. Box section, ladder construction. 2mm (14 swg) steel.
Paint treatment. Zinc phosphate, cathodic electro coat followed by waxing in rear cross member.

SUSPENSION
Standard suspension. Long travel single-rate coil springs, double acting hydraulic dampers.
Front. Beam axle located by radius arms and Panhard rod.
Rear. Beam axle located by trailing links and central A-frame.
High load suspension. As above but with dual rate coil springs on the rear axle.

STEERING
Type. Worm and roller.
Ratio (straight ahead).
Manual: 20.2:1
Power assisted: 19.3:1.
Turns, lock to lock.
Manual: 4.3

Power assisted: 4.0
Wheels. 5.50F x 16 in steel.
6.00JK x 16 styled, optional.
Tyres. See p 108.

BRAKES
Type. Vacuum servo-assisted. 1-1 split dual-circuit hydraulic. Solid disc brakes front and rear.
Handbrake (parking brake). Drum type. Single drum operating on transfer box rear output shaft. Handbrake not for use while vehicle in motion.

...continued

Technical data – Defender 90 – contd

ENGINE – PETROL V8
Type. V8-cylinder, aluminium construction with 5-bearing crankshaft and self-adjusting hydraulic tappets.
Bore. 88.9 mm (3.50 in)
Stroke. 71.12 mm (2.80 in)
Displacement. 3528 cc (215 cu in)
Compression ratio. 8.13:1
Max power. 134 bhp @ 5000 rpm (100 kw) DIN 70020.
Max torque. 187.0 lbf ft @ 2500 rpm (253 Nm).

ENGINE – PETROL 4 CYL
Type. 4 cylinder in-line, cast iron block and cylinder head, 5 bearing crankshaft.
Bore. 90.47 mm (3.56 in)
Stroke. 97.00 mm (3.82 in)
Displacement. 2495 cc (152 cu in)
Compression ratio. 8:1
Max power. 83 bhp @ 4000 rpm (62 kw) DIN Net 70020
Max torque. 133 lbf ft @ 2000 rpm (181 Nm).

ENGINE – DIESEL Tdi
Type. 200Tdi, 4 cylinder in-line, intercooled and turbo-charged high speed direct injection diesel. Cast iron with aluminium cylinder head.
Bore. 90.47 mm (3.56 in)
Stroke. 97.00 mm (3.82 in)
Displacement. 2495 cc (152 cu in)
Compression ratio. 19.5:1
Max power. 107 bhp @ 3800 rpm (80 kw) DIN Net 70020.
Max torque. 188 lbf ft @ 1800 rpm (255 Nm)

Turbo-charger model. Garrett T25.
Maximum operating pressure. 0.8 bar (0.84 kgf/cm^2, 12 lbf/in^2)

ENGINE – DIESEL N/A
(N/A = normally aspirated, ie not turbo-charged)
Type. 4 cylinder in-line. Cast iron block and cylinder head, 5 bearing crankshaft.
Bore. 90.47 mm (3.56 in)
Stroke. 97.00 mm (3.82 in)
Displacement. 2495 cc (152 cu in)
Compression ratio. 21:1
Max power. 68 bhp @ 4000 rpm (51 kw) DIN Net 70020.
Max torque. 117 lbf ft @ 1800 rpm (158 Nm)

FUEL SYSTEM – PETROL V8
Carburettor type. Twin SU HIF44.
Fuel pump. Electrical, submerged in fuel tank.
Filters. In line.
Fuel tank construction. Mild steel, tin terne coated and stitch welded.
Fuel. 91/93 RON leaded, 91/93 RON unleaded.

FUEL SYSTEM – PETROL 4 CYL
Carburettor type. Weber 32/34 DM TL.
Fuel pump. Electrical, submerged in fuel tank.
Filters. In line.
Fuel tank construction. Mild steel, tin terne coated and stitch welded.
Fuel. 90 RON (2 star) leaded 90 RON unleaded.

FUEL SYSTEM – DIESEL Tdi
Injector pump. Bosch KBEL 98 PVI 870398 (2 spring)
Fuel pump. Engine driven mechanical pump.
Fuel tank construction. Mild steel tin terne coated and stitch welded.
Filters. In line filter.
Fuel. Derv class A1 or A2.

FUEL SYSTEM – DIESEL N/A
Type. Self governing DPA distributor type.
Fuel pump. Engine driven mechanical pump.
Fuel tank construction. Mild steel tin terne coated and stitch welded.
Filters. In line filter.
Fuel. Derv class A1 or A2.

COOLING SYSTEM
Type. Pressurised liquid with pump and mechanical fan.
Radiator
Except Tdi – copper and brass full face area type.
Tdi – copper and brass integral unit with oil cooler and aluminium intercooler.
Thermostat
Petrol 4 cyl, diesel N/A – 82°C.
V8 and diesel Tdi – 88°C.
Fan
V8 and diesel Tdi – 406 mm (16 in). Temperature sensitive viscous drive.
Petrol 4 cyl and diesel N/A – 390 mm (15.5 in), 4 blade.

ELECTRICAL SYSTEM
Battery
Petrol – 12v, 9-plate, 55 amp hr.
Diesel – 12v, 14-plate, 95 amp hr
Alternator
Petrol – 65 amp.
Diesel – 65 amp.
Headlamps. 75/50 watt sealed beam units.

TRANSMISSION
Clutch
V8 – 267 mm (10.5 in) diam.
4 cylinder engines – 235 mm (9.25 in) diam, push diaphragm spring. Asbestos-free lining.
Main gearbox. LT77S manual gearbox incorporating five forward speeds and one reverse. Synchromesh on all forward gears.
Transfer gearbox. LT230T 2-speed reduction on main gearbox output. Front and rear drive permanently engaged via a third differential – locked mechanically by movement of the transfer lever to the left.

OVERALL GEAR RATIOS

	V8 pet	4 cyl pet
High range		
5th	3.331:1	4.151:1
4th	4.326:1	4.995:1
3rd	6.043:1	7.527:1
2nd	9.227:1	11.493:1
1st	15.971:1	17.907:1
Reverse	14.833:1	18.486:1
Low range		
5th	9.050:1	9.767:1
4th	11.753:1	11.753:1
3rd	16.419:1	17.711:1
2nd	25.057:1	27.043:1
1st	43.391:1	42.134:1
Reverse	40.300:1	43.497:1

	Diesel Tdi	Diesel N/A
High range		
5th	3.846:1	4.151:1
4th	4.995:1	4.995:1
3rd	6.978:1	7.527:1
2nd	10.649:1	11.493:1
1st	18.441:1	17.907:1
Reverse	17.127:1	18.486:1
Low range		
5th	9.050:1	9.767:1
4th	11.753:1	11.753:1
3rd	16.419:1	17.711:1
2nd	25.057:1	27.043:1
1st	43.391:1	42.497:1
Reverse	40.300:1	43.497:1

FINAL DRIVE

Axle ratios. 3.538:1

Transfer ratios

	V8	All 4 cyl
High	1.222:1	1.411:1
Low	3.220:1	3.320:1

Front axle. Spiral bevel crown wheel and pinion with fully enclosed constant velocity joints.

Rear axle. Spiral bevel crown wheel and pinion with fully floating shafts.

BODY

Material. All panels with the exception of the dash bulkhead are of aluminium alloy. Front wheelarches of galvanised steel.

Plating/painting. Zinc phosphate. Cathodic electrocoat, polyester surfacer. Colour coat – alkyd for solid colours.

Defender 90 hard top

CAPACITIES (litres, Imp gal)

Full fuel tank
54.5 lit (12 gal)

Low fuel warning
9 lit (2 gal)

Cooling system
V8 petrol: 12.8 lit (22.5 pint)
4 cyl petrol: 10.8 lit (19 pint)
Diesel Tdi: 11.1 lit (20 pint)
Diesel N/A: 10.8 lit (19 pint)

Engine oil, including filter
V8 petrol: 5.66 lit (10 pint)
All 4 cyl engines: 6.85 lit (12 pint)

Main gearbox
2.67 lit (4.7 pint)

Transfer gearbox
2.3 lit (4.0 pint)

Front differential
1.7 lit (3.0 pint)

Rear differential
1.7 lit (3.0 pint)

Swivel pin housing
0.35 lit (0.6 pint)

Power steering
2.9 lit (5.0 pint)

Windscreen washer reservoir
2.0 lit (3.5 pint)

TECHNICAL DATA – DEFENDER 110
Pick-ups and soft-top

Weights

Model	110 Soft Top				110 Pick-Up				110 High Capacity Pick-Up			
Engine	2.5P	3.5P	2.5D	2.5Tdi	2.5P	3.5P	2.5D	2.5Tdi	2.5P	3.5P	2.5D	2.5Tdi
Gross vehicle weight kg	Unlevelled suspension: 3050											
Kerb weight kg	1805	1806	1828	1872	1815	1815	1839	1880	1853	1853	1877	1917
Payload kg	1245	1244	1222	1178	1235	1235	1211	1170	1197	1197	1173	1133
Gross vehicle weight kg	Levelled suspension: 2950											
Kerb weight kg	1815	1816	1838	1882	1825	1825	1849	1890	1863	1863	1887	1927
Payload kg	1135	1134	1112	1068	1125	1125	1101	1060	1087	1087	1063	1023
Seating capacity	2/3/11				2/3/11				2/3			

Defender 110 comes in six body options (see p134 for full length hard-tops), each with four engine options, unlevelled or levelled suspension, manual or power assisted steering.

Exterior dimensions – *all* Defender 110 – mm (ins)

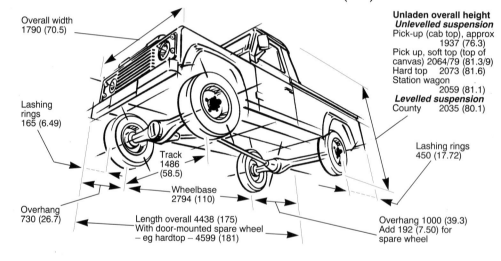

Overall width 1790 (70.5)

Lashing rings 165 (6.49)

Track 1486 (58.5)

Overhang 730 (26.7)

Wheelbase 2794 (110)

Length overall 4438 (175)
With door-mounted spare wheel
– eg hardtop – 4599 (181)

Unladen overall height
Unlevelled suspension
Pick-up (cab top), approx 1937 (76.3)
Pick up, soft top (top of canvas) 2064/79 (81.3/9)
Hard top 2073 (81.6)
Station wagon 2059 (81.1)
Levelled suspension
County 2035 (80.1)

Lashing rings 450 (17.72)

Overhang 1000 (39.3)
Add 192 (7.50) for spare wheel

Wheelbase is exactly 110 inches.

Interior dimensions – 110 std pick-ups, soft tops – mm (ins)

See also p 118 – biggest slide-in box

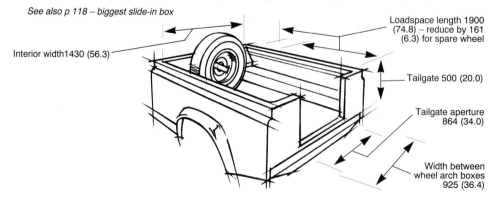

Interior width 1430 (56.3)

Loadspace length 1900 (74.8) – reduce by 161 (6.3) for spare wheel

Tailgate 500 (20.0)

Tailgate aperture 864 (34.0)

Width between wheel arch boxes 925 (36.4)

Length of load space times interior width gives load area of 2.72 sq metres (3.36 sq metres on Hi Cap pick-up opposite).

Defender 110 High Capacity Pick-Up (HCPU) is cleared for slightly higher payload (about 38 kg) than standard version but its main strength is ability to accept far bulkier loads. HCPU left, standard 110 pickup, right.

Exterior dimensions – 110 High Capacity pick-up – mm (ins)

Dimensions differ from 110 standard pickup only in overall length, rear overhang, rear lashing rings, height.

Defender 110's max payloads of 1023-1245 kg (see p 134 for hard-tops) are higher than 90's and give best trade-off of power-weight ratio for load capacity. Hi Cap is optimised for lower-density bulky loads.

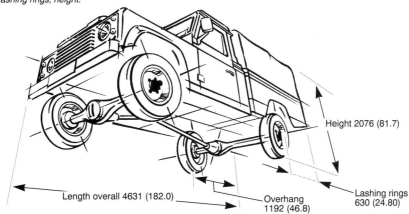

Height 2076 (81.7)

Length overall 4631 (182.0)

Overhang 1192 (46.8)

Lashing rings 630 (24.80)

Loadspace – Defender 110 HCPU – mm (ins)

See also p 119 – biggest slide-in box

Loadspace length 2010 (79.2) – NB Longer than Defender 130 HCPU

Interior width 1670 (65.75)

Width between wheel arches 1090 (43.0)

Beam axles and coil springs front and rear. Disc brakes front and rear, servo assisted. Power assisted steering standard.

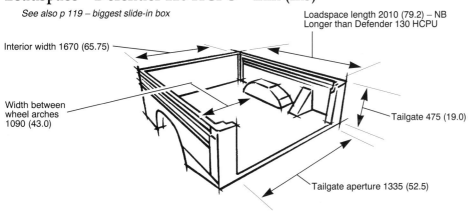

Tailgate 475 (19.0)

Tailgate aperture 1335 (52.5)

...continued

Land Rover Experience

Technical data – Defender 110
Pick-ups and soft top – continued

Geometric limitations

Hi Cap is designed for low-density loads, has full width tailgate, minimal intrusion of wheel arches and can accept 1-metre pallets.

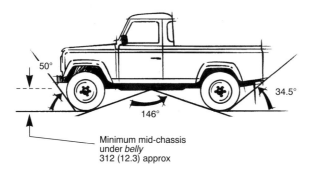

50°   34.5°
146°

Minimum mid-chassis under *belly* 312 (12.3) approx

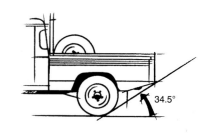

34.5°

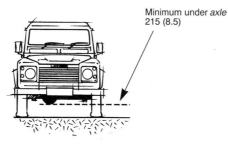

Minimum under *axle* 215 (8.5)

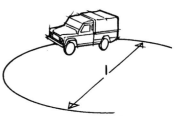

Minimum kerb-kerb turning circle 12.8 m (42.0 ft)

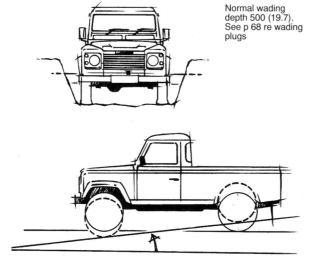

Normal wading depth 500 (19.7). See p 68 re wading plugs

Longitudinal articulation coefficient (see Glossary p 154)
C_{LA}= 12.11

CHASSIS
As Defender 90 – p 127.

SUSPENSION
Type. Long travel coil spring, dual-rate front spring, single rate rear. Double-acting hydraulic dampers.
Front. Beam axle located by radius arms and Panhard rod.
Rear – unlevelled. (3050 kg GVW). Beam axle located by trailing links and central A-frame.
Rear – levelled. (2950 kg GVW). As above plus levelling unit and anti-roll bar.

STEERING
As Defender 90 – p 127.
Wheels. 5.50F x 16 in steel. (Styled steel wheels from Defender 90 not suitable for 110 or 130).
Tyres. 7.50 x 16, see p 109.

BRAKES
As Defender 90 – see p 127.

ENGINES
Petrol V8, 3.5 ltr
Petrol 4 cyl, 2.5 ltr
Diesel Tdi, 2.5 ltr
Diesel N/A, 2.5 ltr
All engines as Defender 90, see
p 128.

FUEL SYSTEMS
All fuel systems as Defender 90
according to engine type – see
p 128. But see below regarding
fuel tank capacity.

COOLING SYSTEMS
All cooling systems as
Defender 90 according to
engine type – see p 128.

ELECTRICAL SYSTEMS
All electrical systems as
Defender 90 – see p 128 –
except headlamps on County
Station Wagon (p 134) which
are halogen 60/55 w.

TRANSMISSION
Transmission system as
Defender 90 – see p 128.

OVERALL GEAR RATIOS

	V8 pet Tdi diesel	4 cyl pet Diesel N/A
High range		
5th	3.846:1	4.903:1
4th	4.995:1	5.901:1
3rd	6.978:1	8.893:1
2nd	10.649:1	13.579:1
1st	18.441:1	21.156:1
Reverse	17.128:1	21.840:1
Low range		
5th	9.050:1	9.767:1
4th	11.753:1	11.753:1
3rd	16.419:1	17.711:1
2nd	25.057:1	27.043:1
1st	43.391:1	42.134:1
Reverse	40.300:1	43.497:1

FINAL DRIVE
Axle ratios. 3.583:1
Transfer ratios

	V8 pet Tdi diesel	4 cyl pet Diesel N/A
High	1.411:1	1.667:1
Low	3.320:1	3.320:1

Front axle, rear axle. As
Defender 90 – see p 129.

BODY
Material and finish. As
Defender 90 – see p 129.

Defender 110 pick-up ..   ... and HCPU (below)

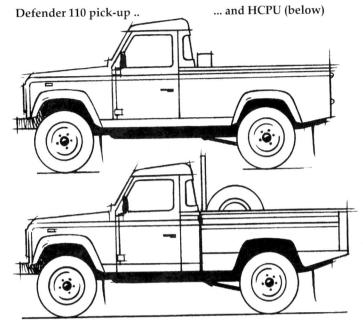

CAPACITIES (litres, Imp gal)
All capacities as Defender 90 –
p 129 – except the following:
Full fuel tank
Standard rear tank 79.5 lit (17.5
gal)
Side tank option – station
wagon only – 45.5 lit (10.0 gal)
Side tank option – others – 68.2
lit (15.0 gal)
Rear differential
2.26 lit (4.0 pint)

*On soft-tops, the side curtains may
be rolled up for easier access to
interior. All pick-ups are available
with three-quarter length canvas
tilt.*

Land Rover Experience

TECHNICAL DATA – DEFENDER 110, 130
Full-length hard-tops, 130 HCPU and crew cab

Weights

Model	110 Hard Top				110 Station Wagon				110 County				130 Crew Cab, HCPU	
Engine	2.5P	3.5P	2.5D	2.5Tdi	2.5P	3.5P	2.5D	2.5Tdi	2.5P	3.5P	2.5D	2.5Tdi	3.5P	2.5Tdi
Gross vehicle weight kg	Unlevelled suspension: 3050													
Kerb weight kg	1840	1840	1867	1913	1943	1944	1969	2018	1979	1980	2005	2054	2012	2086
Payload kg	1210	1210	1183	1137	1107	1106	1081	1032	1071	1070	1045	996	1488	1414
Gross vehicle weight kg	Levelled suspension: 2950													
Kerb weight kg	1850	1850	1877	1923	1953	1954	1979	2028	1989	1990	2015	2064	N/A	N/A
Payload kg	1100	1100	1073	1027	997	996	971	922	961	960	935	886	N/A	N/A
Seating capacity	2/3/11				9/10/11/12				9/10/11/12				5/6/12	

Defender 130, as a production line vehicle, comes with a 6-man crew cab and slightly shortened Hi Cap pick up back end.

Exterior dimensions – Defender 130 (see p 130 for 110) – mm (ins)

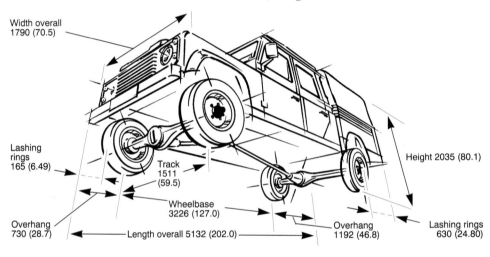

Width overall 1790 (70.5)

Height 2035 (80.1)

Lashing rings 165 (6.49)

Track 1511 (59.5)

Wheelbase 3226 (127.0)

Overhang 730 (28.7)

Length overall 5132 (202.0)

Overhang 1192 (46.8)

Lashing rings 630 (24.80)

It is also available, through Land Rover Special Vehicles as a chassis-cab – 3-man 2-door or 6-man 4-door – with almost any body a customer may require. Engines are V8 or Tdi. Wheelbase is 127 inches.

Loadspace – Defender 130 Crew Cab HCPU – mm (ins)

See also p 119 – biggest slide-in box

Loadspace length 1670 (65.75) – NB Less than 110 HCPU

Interior width 1670 (65.75)

Width between wheel arches 1090 (43.0)

Tailgate 475 (19.0)

Tailgate aperture 1335 (52.5)

Length of load space times interior width gives load area (in the pick up portion) of 1.82 sq metres. Modular body options shown p 136.

Geometric limitations Defender 130 (all 110s on p 132) – mm (ins)

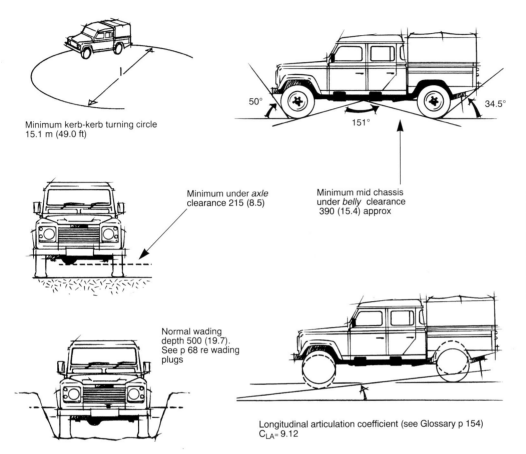

Minimum kerb-kerb turning circle
15.1 m (49.0 ft)

50°

151°

34.5°

Minimum under *axle*
clearance 215 (8.5)

Minimum mid chassis
under *belly* clearance
390 (15.4) approx

Normal wading
depth 500 (19.7).
See p 68 re wading
plugs

Longitudinal articulation coefficient (see Glossary p 154)
C_{LA}= 9.12

*Defender 110 hard
top, estates' payload
is 996-1210 kg.
Production Defender
130s' is over 1400
kg. Special Vehicles
models share same
3500 kg GVW;
payload will vary
with body.*

Interior dimensions – 110 hardtop (see also pp 130) – mm (ins)

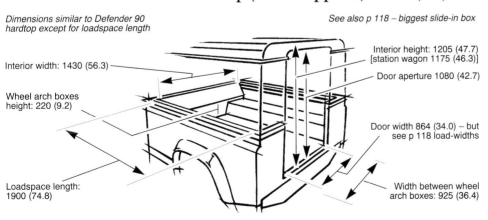

*Dimensions similar to Defender 90
hardtop except for loadspace length*

See also p 118 – biggest slide-in box

Interior width: 1430 (56.3)

Interior height: 1205 (47.7)
[station wagon 1175 (46.3)]

Door aperture 1080 (42.7)

Wheel arch boxes
height: 220 (9.2)

Door width 864 (34.0) – but
see p 118 load-widths

Loadspace length:
1900 (74.8)

Width between wheel
arch boxes: 925 (36.4)

*As with other
Defenders, 130 has
beam axles and coil
springs front and
rear. Disc brakes
front, drums rear,
servo assisted. Power
steering is standard
on 130.*

...continued

Technical data – Defender 110, 130
Full-length hard-tops, 130 HCPU and crew cab – continued

NB Technical data for hard-top Defender 110 in this section is the same as for 110 pick-ups and soft top as shown on pp 132-133. Written data here mainly concerns Defender 130.

CHASSIS
As Defender 90 – see p 127.

SUSPENSION
Defender 110 – see p 132.
Defender 130 – as below:
Type. Long travel coil springs. Single rate front spring. Rear springs comprise two sets of single rate coil springs co-axially mounted each side, one within the other. Double-acting hydraulic dampers.
Front. Beam axle located by radius arms and Panhard rod.
Rear. Beam axle located by trailing links and central A-frame. Unlevelled, with anti-roll bar.

STEERING
Defender 110 – see p 132.
Defender 130:
As Defender 90 – p 127 – but power assisted steering standard.
Wheels. 6.50F x 16 in steel.
Tyres. 7.50 x 16, see p 113.

BRAKES
As Defender 90 – see p 127.

ENGINES
Defender 110 – see p133.
Defender 130:
Petrol V8, 3.5 ltr
Diesel Tdi, 2.5 ltr
Engine details as Defender 90 – see p 128.

FUEL SYSTEMS
Fuel systems as Defender 90 according to engine type – see p 128. But see below regarding fuel tank capacity on 130.

Land Rover Special Vehicles Quadtec modular body system for Defender 130

Quadtec 1 and 2 for 6-man crew-cab

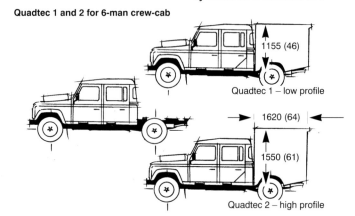

1155 (46)
Quadtec 1 – low profile

1620 (64)
1550 (61)
Quadtec 2 – high profile

Quadtec 3 and 4 for 3-man cab

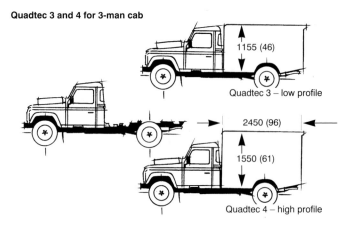

1155 (46)
Quadtec 3 – low profile

2450 (96)
1550 (61)
Quadtec 4 – high profile

COOLING SYSTEMS
Cooling systems as Defender 90 according to engine type – see p 128.

CAPACITIES
As Defender 110 – see p 133.

ELECTRICAL SYSTEM
Defender 110 – see p133.
Defender 130:
As Defender 90 – see p128.

TRANSMISSION
As Defender 90 – see p 128.

GEAR , FINAL DRIVE RATIOS
Defender 110 – see p 133.
Defender 130:
Defender 130 is only fitted with petrol V8 or diesel Tdi engines. Overall and final drive ratios are as for Defender 110 with these engines – see p 133.

BODY
Material and finish. As Defender 90.
Defender 130: Special Vehicles bodies mainly aluminium.

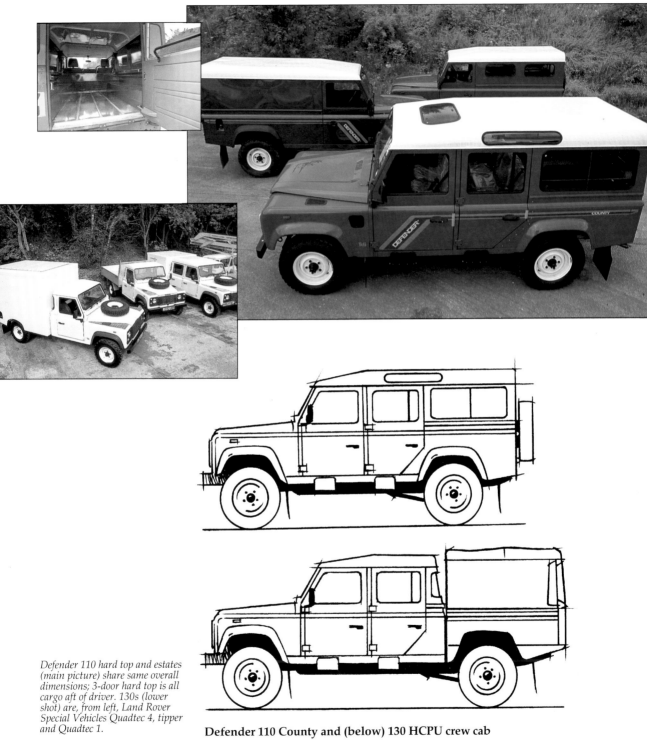

Defender 110 hard top and estates (main picture) share same overall dimensions; 3-door hard top is all cargo aft of driver. 130s (lower shot) are, from left, Land Rover Special Vehicles Quadtec 4, tipper and Quadtec 1.

Defender 110 County and (below) 130 HCPU crew cab

TECHNICAL DATA – DISCOVERY

Weights

Model	3 door				5 door			
Engine	3.5V8	3.9V8	2.5Tdi	2.0Mpi	3.5V8	3.9V8	2.5Tdi	2.0Mpi
Gross vehicle weight kg	All models 2720							
Kerb weight kg	1919	1919	2008	1890	1986	1986	2053	1925
Payload kg	801	801	712	830	734	734	667	795
Seating capacity	5 (7 if optional rear seats fitted)							

Notes:
1. Options affect kerb weight as shown: *adjust payload to keep within GVW*.
   Air conditioning   +42 kg
   Auto transmission, V8, Tdi   -7 kg
   Catalyst on V8 (Std on Mpi) +7 kg
2. Late 1993, 3.5V8i replaced by 3.9V8.

Discovery comes as a 3-door or a 5-door, each with the option of 3.9V8 or 2.0 l petrol or 2.5 l diesel engines. Auto transmission available with V8 and diesel.

Exterior dimensions mm (ins)

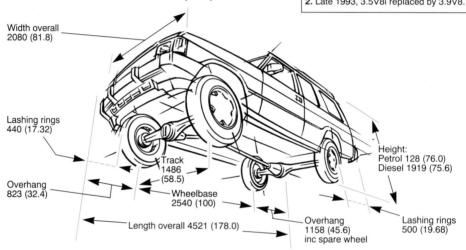

Width overall
2080 (81.8)

Lashing rings
440 (17.32)

Overhang
823 (32.4)

Track
1486
(58.5)

Wheelbase
2540 (100)

Length overall 4521 (178.0)

Height:
Petrol 128 (76.0)
Diesel 1919 (75.6)

Overhang
1158 (45.6)
inc spare wheel

Lashing rings
500 (19.68)

Wheelbase is 100 inches.

Interior dimensions – mm (ins)

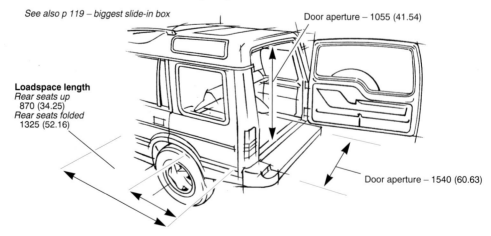

See also p 119 – biggest slide-in box

Door aperture – 1055 (41.54)

Loadspace length
Rear seats up
870 (34.25)
Rear seats folded
1325 (52.16)

Door aperture – 1540 (60.63)

Luggage capacity is 1.29 cu m (45.8 cu ft) seats up, 1.97 cu m (69.8 cu ft) seats down.

Geometric limitations

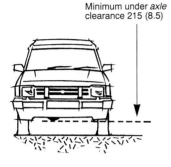

Minimum under *axle* clearance 215 (8.5)

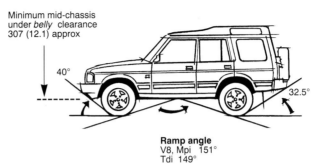

Minimum mid-chassis under *belly* clearance 307 (12.1) approx

40°

32.5°

Ramp angle
V8, Mpi 151°
Tdi 149°

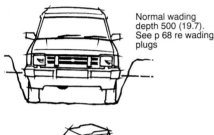

Normal wading depth 500 (19.7). See p 68 re wading plugs

Payload varies between 667 and 830 kg according to body type and engine.

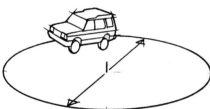

Minimum kerb-kerb turning circle 11.9 m (39.0 ft)

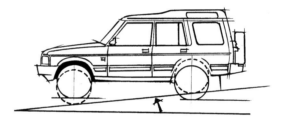

Longitudinal articulation coefficient (see Glossary p 154)
C_{LA}= 14.59

CHASSIS
Type. Box section, ladder construction. 2mm (14 swg) steel.
Paint treatment. Zinc phosphate, cathodic electro coat followed by waxing in the box sections.

SUSPENSION
Type. Long travel coil spring, single rate front, dual rate rear. Double acting hydraulic dampers.
Front. Beam axle located by radius arms and Panhard rod.
Rear. Beam axle located by trailing links and central A-frame.

Levelling and control. Front and rear anti-roll bars optional on all models as part of 'Freestyle Choice' handling package (includes wider 235/70 x 16 tyres); anti-roll bars standard on V8 vehicles from late '93.

STEERING
Type. Power assisted, worm and roller (Adwest Varamatic).
Ratio. Straight ahead – 19.3:1 On lock – 17.2:1
Turns, lock to lock. 3.375.
Wheels.
7.00J x 16 in styled steel (standard, 3 door)
7.00J x 16 in 5-spoke alloy

(optional 3 door, standard 5 door; special style with 'Freestyle Choice' option)..
Tyres. See p 114; tubeless tyres on alloy wheels – see p 115.

BRAKES
Type. Vacuum servo-assisted. IH split dual circuit hydraulic, solid disc brakes front and rear. (Ventilated front discs with asbestos-free pads – certain markets.) Asbestos-free pads on all vehicles from late '93.
Handbrake (parking brake). Single drum operating on transfer box rear output shaft. Handbrake not for use while vehicle in motion.

Beam axles and coil springs front and rear. Disc brakes front and rear, servo assisted. Power steering standard.

...continued

Technical data – Discovery – continued

ENGINE – PETROL V8
Type. V8-cylinder, aluminium construction with 5-bearing crankshaft and self-adjusting hydraulic tappets.
V8 3.9 litre
See p 144. Bore. stroke, power and torque as for Range Rover 3.9 V8. Catalyst standard.
V8 3.5 litre
Bore. 88.9 mm (3.50 in)
Stroke. 71.1 mm (2.80 in)
Displacement. 3528 cc (215 cu in)
High compression, non-catalyst:
Compression ratio. 9.35:1
Max power. 163.6 bhp @ 4750 rpm (122 kw) DIN 70020.
Max torque. 211.9 lbf ft @ 2600 rpm (287.3 Nm).
Low compression, catalyst:
Compression ratio. 8.13:1
Max power. 152.4 bhp @ 4750 rpm (113.6 kw) DIN 70020.
Max torque. 192.3 lbf ft @ 3000 rpm (260.7 Nm).

ENGINE – DIESEL Tdi
Type. 200Tdi, 4 cylinder in-line, intercooled and turbo-charged high speed direct injection diesel. Cast iron with aluminium cylinder head.
Bore. 90.47 mm (3.56 in)
Stroke. 97.00 mm (3.82 in)
Displacement. 2495 cc (152 cu in)
Compression ratio. 19.5:1
Max power. 111.3 bhp @ 4000 rpm (83 kw) DIN Net 70020.
Max torque. 195.5 lbf ft @ 1800 rpm (265 Nm).
Turbo-charger model. Garrett T25.
Maximum operating pressure. 0.8 bar (0.84 kgf/cm^2, 12 lbf/in^2).

ENGINE – PETROL Mpi
Type. 2.0 Mpi, 4 cylinder in-line. Iron block, aluminium head, 16 valves with self-adjusting hydraulic tappets. Twin overhead camshafts, belt driven. Distributor-less, breaker-less quad-coil electronic ignition. Catalyst exhaust standard.
Bore. 84.5 mm (3.33 in)
Stroke. 89.0 mm (3.50 in)
Displacement. 1994 cc (121 cu in)
Compression ratio. 10.0:1
Max power. 134 bhp @ 6000 rpm (100 kw) DIN 70020.
Max torque. 140 lbf ft @ 3600 rpm (190 Nm).

FUEL SYSTEM – PETROL V8
Fuel injection type. Lucas electronic fuel injection with 14CUX-ECU.
Fuel pump. Electrical, submerged in fuel tank.
Filters. In line.
Fuel tank construction. Blow moulded plastic – high density polyurethane.
Fuel. 97 RON leaded, 95 RON unleaded.

FUEL SYSTEM – DIESEL Tdi
Injector pump. Bosch KBEL 98 PVI 870398 (2 spring).
Fuel pump. Engine driven mechanical pump.
Fuel tank construction. Blow moulded plastic – high density polyurethane.
Filters. In line filter.
Fuel. Derv class A1 or A2.

FUEL SYSTEM – PETROL Mpi
As V8 system except:
Fuel injection type. Multi-point electronic fuel injection with MEMS 1.6 fuelling and ignition ECU.
Fuel. 95 RON unleaded.

COOLING SYSTEM
Type. Pressurised liquid with pump and mechanical fan.
Radiator
V8 engine – copper and brass full face area. No oil cooler.
Tdi engine – copper and brass integral unit with oil cooler and aluminium intercooler.
Mpi engine – copper and brass full face area type.
No oil cooler.
Gearbox oil cooler
V8 engine – single air blast.
Tdi and Mpi engine – none.
Thermostat. 88°C.
Fan
V8 – 432 mm (17 in).
Tdi – 406 mm (16 in).
Temperature sensitive viscous drive.
Mpi – single electrically driven 290 mm (11.4 in) fan; twin units when air conditioning fitted .

ELECTRICAL SYSTEM
Battery
V8 and Mpi engine – 12v, 9-plate, 55 amp hr.
Tdi engine – 12v, 14-plate, 72 amp hr.
Alternator
V8 engine – 72 amp (85 amp on 3.9V8).
Tdi engine – 65 amp.
Mpi engine – 100 amp.
Headlamps. 60/55 watt halogen bulbs.

TRANSMISSION
Manual transmission
Clutch
V8 engine – 267 mm (10.5 in) diam.
Tdi engine – 235 mm (9.25 in) diam, push diaphragm spring. Asbestos-free lining.
Mpi engine – 242 mm (9.53 in)
Main gearbox. LT77S manual gearbox incorporating five forward speeds and one reverse. Synchromesh on all forward gears.
Automatic transmission
Automatic gearbox. Available on V8 and Tdi engines only. ZF type 4HP22 with four forward and one reverse speed. Incorporates automatic torque converter lock-up on 4th.
Manual and auto transmission
Transfer gearbox. LT230T 2-speed reduction on main gearbox output. Front and rear drive permanently engaged via a third differential – locked mechanically by movement of the transfer lever to the left.

OVERALL GEAR RATIOS

	V8 manual	V8, Tdi auto
High range		
5th	3.331:1	
4th	4.324:1	3.11:1
3rd	6.040:1	4.27:1
2nd	9.218:1	6.31:1
1st	14.363:1	10.58:1
Reverse	14.827:1	8.89:1
Low range		
5th	9.049:1	
4th	11.747:1	8.36:1
3rd	16.405:1	11.48:1
2nd	25.040:1	17.00:1
1st	39.017:1	28.45:1
Reverse	40.276:1	23.94:1

	Tdi manual	Mpi manual
High range		
5th	3.331:1	3.951:1
4th	4.324:1	4.989:1
3rd	6.040:1	6.959:1
2nd	9.218:1	10.636:1
1st	15.962:1	16.567:1
Rev	14.827:1	17.101:1
Low range		
5th	9.049:1	9.303:1
4th	11.747:1	11.746:1
3rd	16.406:1	16.386:1
2nd	25.040:1	25.043:1
1st	43.367:1	39.009:1
Rev	40.276:1	40.266:1

FINAL DRIVE RATIOS
Axle ratios. 3.538:1
Transfer ratios

	V8,Tdi	Mpi
High	1.222:1	1.410:1
Low	3.220:1	3.320:1

Front axle. Spiral bevel crown wheel and pinion, enclosed constant velocity joints.
Rear axle. Spiral bevel crown wheel and pinion with fully floating shafts.

BODY
Construction. Steel monocoque frame with aluminium alloy body panels (roof panel steel).
Aluminium panels. Front wings, bonnet, body sides, rear quarters, door outer panels.
Plating/painting. Zinc phosphate. Cathodic electrocoat, polyester surfacer. Colour coated either clear over metallic or alkyd solid colours.

Discovery 5-door

CAPACITIES (litres, Imp gal)
Full fuel tank
88.6 lit (19.5 gal)
Usable fuel
81.7 lit (18.0 gal)
Low fuel warning
12 lit approx
Cooling system
V8 – 11.3 lit
Diesel Tdi – 11.5 lit
Mpi – 10 lit
Engine oil, including filter
V8 – 5.66 lit
Diesel Tdi – 6.75 lit
Mpi – 4.5-5.5 lit (min-max)
Main gearbox (manual)

V8 – 3.17 lit
Diesel Tdi and Mpi – 2.67 lit
Main gearbox (auto)
9.8 lit
Transfer gearbox
2.8 lit
Front differential
1.7 lit
Rear differential
1.7 lit
Swivel pin housing
0.36 lit
Power steering
2.9 lit
Windscreen washer reservoir
7.4 lit

TECHNICAL DATA – RANGE ROVER

Weights

Model	2 door 100 inch			4 door 100 inch			4 door LSE 108 inch
Engine	3.9 V8	3.9 V8 Auto	2.5 Tdi	3.9 V8	3.9 V8 Auto	2.5Tdi	4.2 V8 Auto
Gross vehicle weight kg	All 100 inch models: 2510						2620
Kerb weight kg	1931	1962	2035	1967	2011	2070	2150
Payload	579	548	475	543	499	440	470
Seating capacity	All models 4/5 seats						
To kerb wt add 42 kg for air conditioning. Reduce payload to keep within GVW.							

Range Rover comes as a 2-door or a 4-door. The 4-door is also available in long wheelbase format. The long (108 inch) wheelbase (known as Vogue LSE or County LWB – US Spec) has a 4.2 l engine, auto transmission and air suspension as standard.

Exterior dimensions – mm (ins)

External dimensions the same for LSE except :
Wheelbase: 2743 (108)
Overall length: 4648 (183)

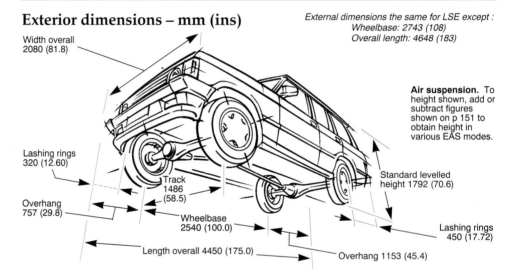

Width overall 2080 (81.8)

Lashing rings 320 (12.60)

Overhang 757 (29.8)

Track 1486 (58.5)

Wheelbase 2540 (100.0)

Length overall 4450 (175.0)

Overhang 1153 (45.4)

Air suspension. To height shown, add or subtract figures shown on p 151 to obtain height in various EAS modes.

Standard levelled height 1792 (70.6)

Lashing rings 450 (17.72)

The Vogue and Vogue SE Range Rover has a 100 inch wheelbase. It is available with a 3.9 l petrol engine or a 2.5 l Tdi diesel. The petrol version is available with auto transmission and air suspension.

Interior dimensions – mm (ins)

See also p 119 - biggest slide-in box

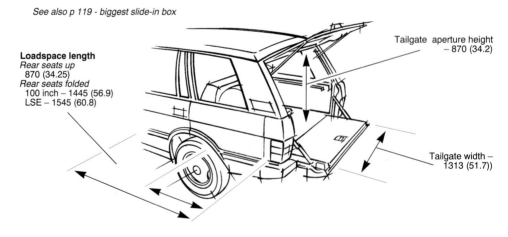

Loadspace length
Rear seats up
870 (34.25)
Rear seats folded
100 inch – 1445 (56.9)
LSE – 1545 (60.8)

Tailgate aperture height – 870 (34.2)

Tailgate width – 1313 (51.7))

Luggage capacity is 1.02 cu m (36.2 cu ft) seats up; with seats down it is 2.00 cu m (70.8 cu ft) on the 100 inch, 2.16 cu m (76.3 cu ft) on the 108 inch.

Geometric limitations

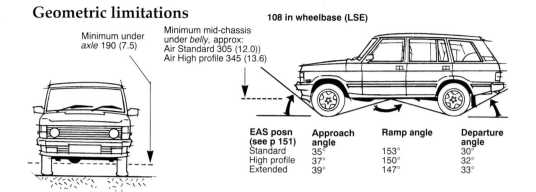

Minimum under *axle* 190 (7.5)

Minimum mid-chassis under *belly*, approx:
Air Standard 305 (12.0))
Air High profile 345 (13.6)

108 in wheelbase (LSE)

EAS posn (see p 151)	Approach angle	Ramp angle	Departure angle
Standard	35°	153°	30°
High profile	37°	150°	32°
Extended	39°	147°	33°

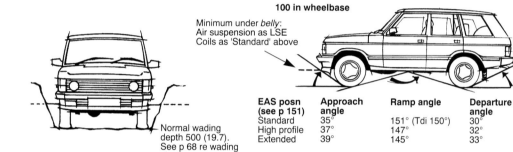

100 in wheelbase

Minimum under *belly*:
Air suspension as LSE
Coils as 'Standard' above

Normal wading depth 500 (19.7).
See p 68 re wading plugs.

EAS posn (see p 151)	Approach angle	Ramp angle	Departure angle
Standard	35°	151° (Tdi 150°)	30°
High profile	37°	147°	32°
Extended	39°	145°	33°

Payload varies between 440 and 579 kg according to body style and engine.

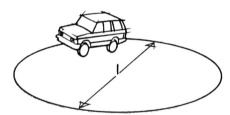
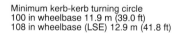

Minimum kerb-kerb turning circle
100 in wheelbase 11.9 m (39.0 ft)
108 in wheelbase (LSE) 12.9 m (41.8 ft)

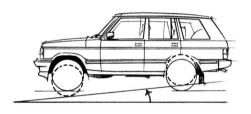

Longitudinal articulation coefficient (see Glossary p 154)
100 inch wheelbase: C_{LA}= 14.59
108 inch wheelbase: C_{LA}= 12.39

Beam axles front and rear with coil springs or air suspension, both self-levelled. Disc brakes front and rear, with ABS and ETC option. Power steering standard.

CHASSIS
Type. Box section, ladder construction. 2mm (14 swg) steel.
Paint treatment. Zinc phosphate, cathodic electro coat followed by waxing in the box sections.

SUSPENSION
Type. Long travel single rate coil springs (standard), or (optional) electronically controlled, variable-height air suspension. Double acting hydraulic dampers.
Front. Beam axle located by radius arms and Panhard rod.
Rear. Beam axle located by trailing links and central A-frame.
Levelling and control
Standard suspension
Self-energising Boge ride-levelling unit fitted to rear axle. Front and rear anti-roll bars standard on Vogue.
Air suspension (LSE, SE , option on Vogue). See p 151.
Variable rate air springs. System activated by electric compressor with pressure reservoir. Four selectable ride heights – normal, low, high and kneel. Auto selection of low above 50 mph (unless manually inhibited), automatic reversion to normal setting at given speeds. Automatic self levelling front and rear. Ride height sensors fitted to radius arms. Front and rear anti-roll bars.

...continued

Technical data – Range Rover – continued

STEERING

Type. Power assisted, worm and roller (Adwest Varamatic).
Ratio.
Straight ahead – 19.3:1
On lock – 14.3:1
Turns, lock to lock. 3.375.
Wheels.
6.00JKJ x 16 in styled steel (standard model)
7.00J x 16 in alloy (Vogue, and SE).
Tyres. See p 114; tubeless tyres on alloy wheels – see p 115.

BRAKES

Type. Vacuum servo-assisted. IH split dual circuit hydraulic, solid disc brakes front and rear. Ventilated front discs with asbestos-free pads front and rear.
Anti-lock brakes (ABS). Electrically driven hydraulic pump and reservoir provide power for electronic 4-channel anti-lock braking system usable on and off-road. ABS standard on Vogue SE and LSE models, optional on others.
Handbrake (parking brake). Single drum operating on transfer box rear output shaft. Handbrake not for use while vehicle in motion.

ENGINE – V8 4.2 litre

Type. V8-cylinder, aluminium construction with 5-bearing crankshaft, self-adjusting hydraulic tappets and fuel injection. Exhaust catalyst standard.
Bore. 94.0 mm (3.70 in)
Stroke. 77 mm (3.03 in)
Displacement. 4278 cc (261 cu in)
Compression ratio. 8.94:1
Max power. 200 bhp @ 4750 rpm (149 kw) DIN 70020.
Max torque. 250 lbf ft @ 3250 rpm (340 Nm).

ENGINE – V8 3.9 litre

Type. V8-cylinder, aluminium construction with 5-bearing crankshaft, self-adjusting hydraulic tappets and fuel injection. Exhaust catalyst standard.
Bore. 94.0 mm (3.70 in)
Stroke. 71.1 mm (2.80 in)
Displacement. 3947 cc (241 cu in)
Compression ratio. 9.35:1
Max power. 181.6 bhp @ 4750 rpm (135.5 kw) DIN 70020.
Max torque. 231.5 lbf ft @ 2600 rpm (314 Nm).

ENGINE – DIESEL Tdi

As Discovery – see p 140.

FUEL SYSTEM – PETROL

As Discovery – see p 140.

FUEL SYSTEM – DIESEL Tdi

As Discovery – see p 140.

COOLING SYSTEM

Type. Pressurised liquid with pump and mechanical fan.
Radiator, oil coolers
V8 auto – copper and brass full face area type with twin oil coolers and single air blast gearbox oil cooler.
V8 manual – copper and brass full face area type with single oil cooler and single air blast gearbox oil cooler..
Tdi engine – copper and brass integral unit with oil cooler and aluminium intercooler.
Thermostat. 88°C.
Fan
V8 – 432 mm (17 in).
Tdi – 406 mm (16 in).
Temperature sensitive viscous drive.

ELECTRICAL SYSTEM

Battery - 12 volt
V8 engine – 9-plate, 55 amp hr.
Tdi engine - 14-plate, 72 amp hr.
Alternator
V8 engine – 85 amp on 3.9, 100 amp on 4.2.
Tdi engine – 65 amp.
NB. 80 amp alternator used when air conditioning fitted.
Headlamps. 60/55 watt halogen bulbs.

TRANSMISSION

Manual transmission
Clutch
V8 engine- 267 mm (10.5 in) diam.
Tdi engine- 235 mm (9.25 in) diam, push diaphragm spring. Asbestos-free lining.
Main gearbox. LT77S manual gearbox incorporating five forward speeds and one reverse. Synchromesh on all forward gears.
Automatic transmission
Automatic gearbox. Available on V8 engines only. ZF type 4HP22 with four forward and one reverse speed. Incorporates automatic torque converter lock-up on 4th.
Manual and auto transmission
Transfer gearbox. Borg Warner type 13-61-000-003 2-speed reduction on main gearbox output. Front and rear drive permanently engaged via a third differential – locked automatically by a viscous coupling unit (VCU) when front/rear prop shaft speed differences are sensed.
Electronic traction control – ETC
ETC is available on vehicles fitted with ABS. A spinning rear wheel is pulse braked to restore overall traction.

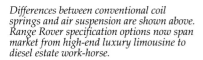

Differences between conventional coil springs and air suspension are shown above. Range Rover specification options now span market from high-end luxury limousine to diesel estate work-horse.

OVERALL GEAR RATIOS

	V8 3.9/4.2 auto	V8 3.9 manual
High range		
5th	-	3.12:1
4th	3.11.1	4.27:1
3rd	4.27:1	5.97:1
2nd	6.32:1	9.10:1
1st	10.59:1	14.18:1
Reverse	8.91:1	14.64:1
Low range		
5th	-	8.40:1
4th	8.36:1	11.48:1
3rd	11.48:1	16.05:1
2nd	17.00:1	24.49:1
1st	28.48:1	38.14:1
Reverse	23.96:1	39.38:1

	Diesel Tdi manual
High range	
5th	3.29:1
4th	4.27:1
3rd	5.97:1
2nd	9.10:1
1st	15.76:1
Reverse	14.64:1
Low range	
5th	8.84:1
4th	11.48:1
3rd	16.04:1
2nd	24.49:1
1st	42.40:1
Reverse	39.38:1

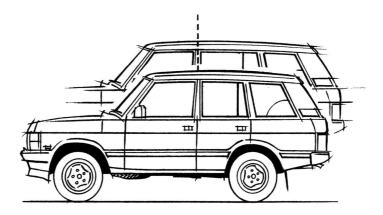

Range Rover 100 inch wheelbase 4-door (108 inch above)

FINAL DRIVE
Axle ratios. 3.540:1
Transfer ratios
High   1.2060:1
Low   3.2444:1
Axles. As Discovery – see p 141.

BODY
Construction. Steel monocoque, bonnet, tailgate, and rear lower quarter panels.
Aluminium panels. Both front wings, roof, body sides, decker and upper rear quarters. All door outer panels.
Plating/painting. Zinc phosphate. Cathodic electrocoat, polyester surfacer. Colour coated either clear over metallic or alkyd for solid colours.

CAPACITIES (litres, Imp gal)
As Discovery – p 141 – except:
Engine oil, including filter
V8 – 6.66 lit
Diesel Tdi – 6.85 lit
Transfer gearbox
1.7 lit

GLOSSARY
and
INDEX
section

GLOSSARY

ABS. Anti-lock braking system; prevents wheels locking under maximum braking. Works on the principle of braking a wheel until it just begins to skid (this is the point where braking efficiency would drop off dramatically) and then releasing the brake pressure and re-applying the brakes. Wheel speed sensors identify the skid point and trigger a release in brake pressure. The cycle is repeated many times a second – with appropriate 'cobblestone' feed-back on the brake pedal to indicate you are in ABS mode. See also 'Cadence braking'.

Air suspension. – see EAS.

Anti-lock brakes. See ABS above.

Approach angle. In side-view, the angle between the ground and a line, ahead of the vehicle, joining the periphery of the front wheel and (typically) the front bumper or other low component. It represents the size or steepness of a slope or obstacle that can be approached or climbed without striking bodywork. See p 30.

Articulation. The ability of one axle to move – left wheel up, right wheel down or vice versa – relative to the chassis or its fellow axle. It is a measure of the ease with which wheels can stay in contact with the ground – and thus retain traction – on very 'twisty' off-road terrain. See p 32, 80.

Articulation angle, longitudinal. See 'Longitudinal articulation angle', p 154.

Axles, one-piece, live. Also referred to as rigid axles, in which the drive shafts to the wheels run within rigid casings without joints to allow vertical hinging as with independent suspension. In an off-road vehicle rigid axles have the advantage of maintaining maximum under-axle ground clearance at all times and always keeping the tyre tread flat on the ground.

Bridle. A rope or cable attached to two points – typically the right and left chassis members – of a vehicle and converging to a point of attachment for a tow rope. See p 82.

Cadence braking. A method of manual braking with the foot brake to simulate the action of ABS brakes – see above. Very effective in slippery conditions where brake locking has occurred or might otherwise occur, the driver applies the footbrake in a series of very rapid jabs at the pedal taking the wheels up to the point of brake locking and then releasing them before the inevitable fall-off in braking efficiency takes place. Effects improved braking in any extremely slippery conditions such as ice, snow, wet mud, or rain. See pp 28, 72, 100.

Capstan winch. A winch, generally mounted on or just behind the front bumper, usually run from an engagable extension to the engine crankshaft. The active component is usually a slowly revolving drum, about 15 cm in diameter, round which a rope may be wound to effect a winching operation. Has the advantage of being powered by the engine at idling speed and being a very low-stress unit that may be used all day without overheating or high electrical load. See p 90.

Castor (or caster) angle. When the front wheels are moved right or left to steer the vehicle they each move about a steering axis. The aft inclination of this steering axis from the vertical (when viewed from the side) – about 3° in the case of most Land

Rovers – is the castor angle. Like casters on a tea trolley or office chair, this puts the ground contact point of the wheels behind the pivot axis and the result is a self-centring action tending to keep the front wheels pointing forward when in forward motion. Note that in deep sand with a 'bow wave' build-up of sand ahead of the wheels the effective ground contact point moves ahead of the steering axis and can give the effect of negative castor with 'runaway' steering. The same thing happens when vehicle is travelling in reverse – the ground contact point being 'ahead' of the steering axis and again tending to make the front wheels 'run away' to full lock – see p 50, failed climbing of steep off-road inclines. Also see 'Steering feel', p 157

Castor action. Tendency of front wheels to self-centre when the steering wheel is released with the vehicle going forward. NB Opposite action takes place when in reverse – see Castor angle above. Castor action is a basic ingredient of steering feel – see 'Steering feel', p 157.

Centre differential. A differential gear

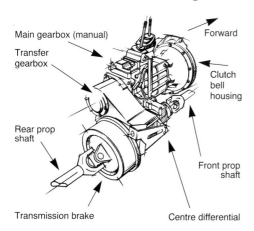

Main gearbox (manual)

Transfer gearbox

Rear prop shaft

Transmission brake

Forward

Clutch bell housing

Front prop shaft

Centre differential

device – diagram p 14 – installed at the point where the transfer box splits engine power between the front and rear axles via the front and rear propeller shafts. Working in the same way as the conventional rear axle differential on a two-wheel drive car, it allows differential rotation of front and rear shafts to accommodate the small rotational differences encountered in normal running, going round sharp corners etc. Such a device is essential in a vehicle having – for use on-road as well as off-road – full-time or permanent 4x4. Vehicles (currently by other manufacturers) fitted with part-time or selectable 4x4 are not fitted with centre differentials and thus cannot be used in four wheel drive on hard roads. See pp 14, 22, also 'Diff lock', p 150.

Chott. Local name for salt flat or sebkha in Tunisia, Algeria and Morocco.

Continuous rolling contact. Description of a wheel in steady rolling contact with the ground without slip, wheel-spin or slide (as with locked brakes). Should be the aim at all times both on and off road. See p 28. Also see 'Discontinuity of rolling contact' below.

Cross-axled. See 'Diagonal suspension'.

Cross ply tyre. Tyre in which the sidewall reinforcement plies run diagonally from the bead towards the tread – each layer of textile at a different angle to its adjacent layer. Generally superseded by radial-ply tyres whose thinner, more flexible sidewalls and braced tread yield better grip and lower rolling resistance. Because of thicker, multi-ply sidewalls, not so prone to sidewall damage as radials and – see pp 65 and 109 – can have low-cost applications when operating continuously on rock. However, reduced pressures in soft going can, due to the thick sidewalls, cause overheating and possibly de-lamination of the tyre. See 'Radial ply tyres' on p 155.

...continued

Glossary – continued

Co-ordinated tow. When recovering a stuck vehicle, the process by which the engine power of both the tug and the stuck vehicle are co-ordinated – usually by a signal from an external marshaller – and the clutches of both vehicles are engaged at the same time to enhance the chance of a first-time recovery. See p 84.

Corrugations. Deformation of an unsurfaced track taking the form of transverse, close-pitch undulations – ie at right angles to the direction of the track. Sometimes referred to as 'washboard'. See p 66.

Coupled brakes. Brake system installed with certain large trailers whereby the trailer brakes are applied at the same time as are the brakes of the towing vehicle. Vehicles must be specifically modified to operate this system – with appropriate trailers. See p 38.

Departure angle. In side view, the angle between the ground and a line, aft of the vehicle, joining the periphery of the rear wheel and (typically) the rear chassis member or other low component. It represents the size or steepness of a slope or obstacle that can be approached or climbed in reverse without striking bodywork. See p 30.

Diagonal suspension. A manifestation occurring off-road when a vehicle is, for example, diagonally crossing a small but well-defined ridge. When the ridge is so severe that, say, the right front wheel and the rear left wheels are on full 'bump' (ie fully up in the wheel arches) and the other wheels are hanging down to the full extent of wheel travel, the vehicle may be described as being diagonally suspended or on diagonal suspension. Some also refer to this state as being 'cross-axled'. See p 46.

Diagonal wheel-spin. The wheel-spin that can take place on the fully extended wheels in a condition of diagonal suspension as described above. However, a vehicle need not be in a totally diagonal suspension condition for diagonal wheel-spin to take place; minor off-loading of diagonally opposed wheels or the presence of slippery ground under these wheels can provoke the condition. Can also occur crossing ditches diagonally; see p 46.

Diff-lock. See first 'Centre differential' above. Locking of the centre differential, activated by moving the transfer gearbox lever to the left and confirmed by illumination of the 'DIFF-LOCK' indicator light, puts the differential function on hold. Where traction conditions or grip are different front and rear there would be a tendency for the centre differential to permit the front wheels, say, to spin ineffectively while they are on wet clay and cause the rear wheels, on grippier ground, to stop rotating. The diff-lock locks the centre differential, thus locking front and rear prop shafts together, ensuring they revolve at the same speed and enhancing traction. Diff-lock is usually engaged for difficult off-road conditions but should *never remain engaged on hard grippy roads.* See also 'Centre differential lock', p 22. See also 'Viscous coupling', p 159.

Differential casing. Not to be confused with the centre differential, each axle, of course, has a normal cross-axle differential at the point where the propeller shaft from the transfer gearbox meets the axle. The size of the crown wheel and pinion plus differential demands a bulge in the axle casing – referred to as the diff casing. It has special significance in off-road vehicles because it is the lowest point of the axle and thus the point of least ground clearance – see p 31.

Discontinuity of rolling contact. Generic term for wheel-spin and wheel slide – as on locked brakes. See 'Continuous rolling contact' above and p 28.

EAS – electronic air suspension.
Introduced in the 1993 model year on certain Range Rover models further to enhance standards of road noise insulation, ride and handling, the system substitutes air bags and a live-line pneumatic system, (ie an electrically driven compressor, air pressure reservoir and associated controls) for the steel coil springs used on the rest of the Land Rover model range. Logic-

controlled by an electronic control unit, height sensors and driver controls, the system maintains front and rear self-levelling in the five height modes listed below. These notes show the versatility of the system and the purpose for which it was designed. However, for the casual driver, new to the vehicle, no prior knowledge or expertise is required; EAS will cycle automatically through appropriate modes according to prior programming. The driver need not even know EAS is fitted. On engine start-up EAS assumes the last selected ride height.

1. *Standard ride height* – similar to that of coil springs; normal road use.

...continued

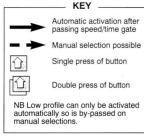

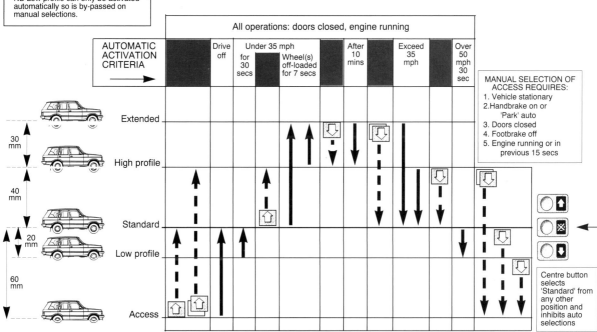

Glossary – continued

2. *Low profile*; automatically activated (unless manually inhibited) to drop ride height by 20 mm if 50 mph is exceeded for 30 seconds. If less than 35 mph is held for more than 30 seconds, standard ride height will be resumed automatically.

3. *High profile*; manually selected by Up button, it raises ride height by 40 mm for use off-road or when wading; auto-reversion to Standard ride height when 35 mph exceeded. May also be manually de-selected.

4. *Access;* manually selected by Down button when stationary and doors closed. Drops ride height by 60 mm from standard. Mode cancelled and standard ride height selected automatically when handbrake released and vehicle driven away. Various requirements – see diagram – before access position can be assumed. Opening a door during descent/ascent to/from Access position will freeze the suspension at that point.

5. *Extended;* raises ride height up to 30 mm above High Profile. Selected automatically when one or more wheels is off-loaded (eg when vehicle is bellied on a mound) for more than 7 seconds. Cannot be selected manually. Suspension reverts to High profile automatically after 10 minutes or reverts to standard ride height if 35 mph is exceeded. May be *de*-selected manually by one or two presses of suspension Down button which will respectively lower it to the High profile or Standard position.

Electronic traction control – ETC. ETC is a standard/optional feature, available only on ABS-equipped Range Rovers. It inhibits wheel-spin by applying brake to a spinning rear wheel and thus enhances traction on ice, snow or in severe off-road conditions. It utilises ABS sensors for wheel speed determination and brakes the spinning wheel to, through the axle differential, apply torque to the stationary wheel. Like ABS, it is especially effective in maintaining control when one side of the vehicle is on a more slippery surface than the other – a so-called 'split-µ' surface. A dashboard light illuminates when the system is operating. The function is inhibited above 50 kph, a speed above which unintentional wheel spin is unlikely to occur. See pp 19, 28.

Engine braking. Vehicle retardation derived from engaging a low gear and taking your foot off the throttle. See also pp 52, 100.

Emergency flotation (pressure). Very low tyre pressure (about 60% of normal road pressures), always associated with a low maximum permitted speed (20 kph or 12 mph) used for traversing or recovery from very soft ground. Such low pressures cause extreme tyre sidewall flexing – hence the speed limitation. See pp 56–59 and pp 112–114.

Emergency soft. Another name for emergency flotation tyre pressure – see above.

ETC . See 'Electronic traction control' above.

Fatigue life. Number of specified load reversals at which a metal component will fail. In the context of this book see fatigue life of nylon snatch-towing ropes – 'Recovery – snatch-towing', p 86.

Fesh-fesh. Desert terrain comprising a thin crust of fine gravel or wind-blown sand laid over deep very fine dust of powder consistency. Can be bad enough to bog a vehicle. Difficult to spot due to overlay of normal-looking sand.

Flotation. Characteristic of a vehicle, by reason of large softly inflated tyres, not to sink on soft going such as mud or sand. See pp 56, 60 and 'Optimum pressures', p 112.

Four-wheel drive (4x4). Vehicle transmission system in which engine power is applied to all four wheels. The term 4x4 (four by four) has the specific connotation that it is a *four* (wheeled vehicle driven) *by four* (wheels). See Section 1, p 10

Full-time 4x4. A transmission system on a four-wheeled vehicle in which all four wheels are driven by the engine all the time. (As opposed to a vehicle that is normally in two-wheel drive with four-wheel drive selected by a separate lever when required.) See pp 10, 18.

Geometric limitations. A term coined for this book to describe the limitations and extent of approach and departure angles, ramp angle, steering lock, articulation and – an even newer term – longitudinal articulation angle. See 'Geometric limitations', p 30 and p 127 et seq.

Ground clearance. Space between the ground and a given mechanical part of the vehicle. Usually, when quoted for a vehicle, taken as the least for any component on the vehicle – the space under the differential casing. But note difference between under-*axle* and under-*belly* clearance – see p 31.

Ground stress. Term coined for this book to indicate how much strength is being asked of a particular piece of ground in terms of flotation or lateral shear to accommodate traction, braking or acceleration. See pp 12, 56.

GVW. Gross vehicle weight – the maximum permitted laden weight of a vehicle including payload, fuel and driver.

Handbrake. See 'Transmission brake'.

Harmonics. Here taken as relating to the natural frequency of a vehicle's suspension system that can influence the formation of transverse surface corrugations on unsurfaced tracks. See p 66.

Heel and toe wear. Jargon for the uneven front to rear wear on individual blocks of a bold off-road tyre tread when used on roads. See p 109, 'Mud tyre' and 'Sand tyre'.

High box. Status of the transmission when the two-speed transfer gearbox lever is in the high ratio position – for normal, on-road, day-to-day use. See p 13.

High ratio. Term to describe the transmission when the transfer gearbox lever is in the high position – high box above.

Hi-lift jack. Versatile lever-operated mechanical bumper jack capable of a lift of a metre or more. See 'Self-recovery', p 81.

Hi-lo lever. Term sometimes used to describe the transfer gearbox lever. See p 13.

High Load suspension. An option on the Defender 90 enabling payload to be raised by about 150 kg – see p 126.

Kerb weight. Unladen weight, ie empty vehicle plus full fuel plus 75 kg driver.

KERR. Kinetic Energy Recovery Rope. Descriptive term coined to describe specially specified nylon ropes capable of stretching during snatch tow. See 'Recovery – snatch-towing', p 86.

Kinetic energy. Energy of motion, proportional to the total weight of the vehicle and the square of its speed. Thus if a vehicle's weight doubles its KE also goes up two times; but if its speed doubles its KE increases by two squared, ie four times. See 'Recovery – snatch-towing', p 86.

...continued

Glossary – continued

Laden. Vehicle carrying some or full payload. See also GVW above concerning loading to maximum permitted weight.

Unlevelled rear suspension

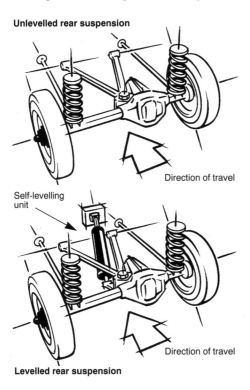

Direction of travel

Self-levelling unit

Direction of travel

Levelled rear suspension

Levelled suspension. (See diagram above.) A means of eliminating the 'squat' of the rear suspension under load by a hydraulic self-levelling unit between the chassis and the centre of the rear axle. Standard on coil sprung Range Rovers, Defender 110 Station Wagons and County; special order on any other Defender 110. See 'Unlevelled suspension', p 159. (Range Rovers with EAS have auto levelling front and rear.)

Longitudinal articulation coefficient – C_{LA}. A single number that conveys the off-road, 'twisty ground' potential of an off-road vehicle. A given max wheel movement enhances this capability more on a short wheelbase than on a long wheelbase

vehicle. C_{LA} is a non-dimensional parameter, provisionally coined, (higher values mean better articulation) that takes account of both wheel movement and wheelbase; it relates to the angle between the ground and a line joining the front and rear hubs (or tyre periphery) when one wheel is on full bump and the other fully

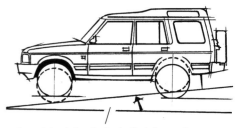

C_{LA} relates to longitudinal articulation angle

extended. Vehicle values pp 127-143.

Low box. Status of the transmission when the transfer gearbox lever is in the low position – for difficult off-road conditions demanding greater traction or low speed control. See 'Traction – extra gears', p 13, and 'Low box – when and how', p 20.

Low ratio. Term to describe the transmission when transfer gearbox lever is in the low position. See pp 18, 20, 22.

Marshalling. ('Marshaller' derived from ground-crew who marshal aircraft on airport aprons.) In the context of off-road operations, taken to mean the detailed direction of a vehicle by a marshaller outside the vehicle who is able to see all four wheels and also the difficult ground being traversed. Marshalling should be undertaken when there is the danger of damaging tyre sidewalls or the underside of the vehicle on rocks or other obstacles. See 'Look before you leap', p 34.

Mechanical sympathy. In the context of this book, concern for and empathy with the structural stress, durability of, and possible damage to mechanical components of your vehicle. In a phrase, caring about your Land Rover. See 'Mind-set – mechanical sympathy', p 26.

M+S tyres. Mud and snow tyres. A generic term for 4x4 tyres with a road-oriented, not especially bold, tread pattern suitable for mild snow and mud conditions. See Section 7, 'Tyres', p 109.

Mud tyres. Bold, open-tread tyres optimised for mud with disadvantages on hard roads. See Section 7, 'Tyres', p 109.

Multi-purpose tyre.
Combination/compromise between on-road and mud tyres. See , 'Tyres', p 109.

NATO towing hook. Large, robust, four-bolt attachment towing pintle with top-closure and, usually, 360° rotational capability about the longitudinal axis originally specified for NATO 7.5 tonne military vehicles. Suitable for off-road towing albeit, due to the fact that a trailer towing eye will not be a close fit over the hook, it generates quite a bit of 'goods train' fore and aft banging. See 'Towing – on-road', p 38 and 'Towing off-road', p 102.

Nose load. Trailers should be nose heavy; the nose-load is the amount of nose-heaviness (sometimes called trailer 'preponderance') measured at the tow-hitch and must be considered part of the towing vehicle's payload. See 'Towing – on-road', p 38.

On-foot recce. Inspecting a difficult off-road obstacle on foot before committing your vehicle to it. See 'Look before you leap', p 34.

Overrun brakes. Trailer brakes activated by the tendency of the trailer to overtake – or overrun – the towing vehicle when the vehicle brakes or slows down. See 'Towing-on-road', p 38.

Over-torque. Used in this book to convey the concept of applying too much torque

(or power) to the wheels so that they break their grip with the ground and spin.

Part-time 4x4. See 'Selectable four-wheel drive' next page.

Permanent four-wheel drive. See 'Full-time 4x4' above.

Radial ply tyre. A type of tyre construction in which sidewall structural plies run radially out towards the tread instead of criss-cross diagonally. With their thinner, more flexible sidewalls, radial tyres have lower rolling resistance than cross-ply tyres (yielding better fuel consumption) as well as giving longer tread life. They can accommodate the use of low inflation pressures without overheating, due to their flexible sidewalls, but are sometimes more

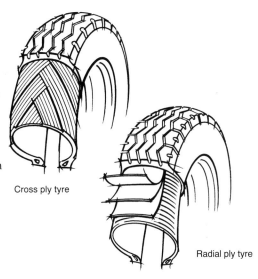

Cross ply tyre

Radial ply tyre

prone to sidewall damage when operating in rocky or stony conditions. Because radial tyres invariably also have a braced tread area of great dimensional stability, they 'track-lay' the tread (like a bulldozer), do not suffer from 'tread shuffle' and so achieve more traction in limiting off-road conditions. See also p 58.

...continued

Glossary – continued

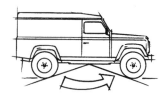

Ramp angle. A measure of vehicle under-belly clearance or the ability to drive over a sharp ridge or ramp without touching the underside of the vehicle on the obstacle. The ramp angle is the angle measured from the lowest part of the chassis at mid-wheelbase down to the periphery of front and rear wheels. Obviously a short wheelbase vehicle with large wheels will have the smallest ramp angle and best under-belly clearance; a Defender 90 will be better than a Defender 130 in this respect. See p 30.

Ramp breakover angle. The fuller title of 'Ramp angle ' above.

Range change. Term sometimes used for the transfer gearbox lever. See p 18.

Reduced inflation. Lowering tyre pressures to increase flotation in soft ground conditions such as mud or soft sand. See p 56 and Section 7, 'Tyres', p 108 et seq.

Rolling contact – see 'Continuous rolling contact'.

Sand ladders. A pair of aluminium ladders, about 170 cm long, specially made with rungs closer than normal, to lay beneath the vehicle wheels in soft sand to give grip and flotation. See 'Self-recovery', p 78.

Sand tracks. Generic name sometimes given to any item fulfilling the role of a sand ladder. May be PSP (pierced steel planking). See 'Self-recovery', p 78 and diagram p 79.

Sand channels. Term often interchangeable with sand tracks, derivative from the days when metal channels were used for this purpose. Can include articulated sand planks, see 'Self-recovery', p 78 and photo p 79.

Sand tyres. Term often used to mean *desert* tyre – implying an ability to cope with desert rock and stones as well as sand. These tyres are characterised by tread blocks of a gentle, shouldered profile with no bold, right-angled edges such as a mud tyre would have. Radial construction is far more suited to the low inflation pressures sometimes used in sand. Despite their appearance, 'balloon' tyres with circumferential groove treads are considerably less effective in sand than a radial such as the Michelin XS. See p 63 and Section 7, 'Tyres', p 108. et seq.

Salt flat. Salt marsh of very unreliable consistency and bearing strength found in desert regions and characterised by a top crust of varying thickness and strength with soft salt mud of great depth beneath it. See p 62, also Chott and Sebkha.

Sebkha. See Salt flat above.

Selectable four-wheel drive. A four-wheeled vehicle which proceeds normally in two-wheel drive but on which, by means of a lever control, four-wheel drive may be selected. It is important to remember that such vehicles in four-wheel drive do not have the benefit of a centre differential (see p 149 above) so should not be used on hard roads or firm grippy surfaces in this mode. See p 14.

Self centring. The characteristic of front (steered) wheels to resume the straight-ahead position due to castor angle (See 'Castor angle', p 148 above) when the steering wheel is released. This characteristic can be utilised to enhance safety when driving in deep wheel ruts on slippery ground. See 'Driving on tracks', p 42 and 'Steering feel' next page.

Self-levelling suspension. See 'Levelled suspension' p 154.

Sidewall. The external 'walls' of a tyre between the tread and the bead or wheel rim. This area is particularly vulnerable on radial ply tyres to damage in off-road operations from oblique rubbing contact with side-swiping sharp rocks. Driver awareness essential. See p 65.

Sidewall awareness. Awareness by sensitive drivers of the susceptibility to damage of the tyre sidewall. An attribute worth developing. See 'Rocks, stones, corrugations', p 65.

Sidewall deflection. Outward movement of the tyre sidewall in the region of the ground contact patch due to low inflation pressures or hitting a sharp bump with

Top section

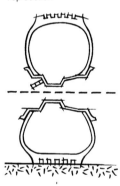

Ground level section

excess speed. It is important not to run tyres at less than recommended inflation pressures for given maximum speeds and loads (see Section 7, 'Tyres', p 108 et seq) since by doing so you will exceed the manufacturer's specified limits for sidewall deflection and thus cause overheating and serious damage to the tyre.

Shock loading. In the context of this book, taken to mean the arrest of mechanical motion in an excessively abrupt way or the application of sharp load reversals in a such a way as to risk structural failure. For example, the application of the handbrake whilst the vehicle is in motion – important, see 'Traction controls', p 19 – can cause unacceptable shock loading of the rear axle half-shafts. (See 'Transmission brake' next

page.) Engaging diff lock whilst one or more wheel is spinning could also result in severe and damaging shock load to the transmission (See also 'Viscous coupling' p 157 and 'Mechanical sympathy', p 154.)

Small gear lever. Don't be embarrassed if you can't remember the name for the transfer gear lever..! (See p 158.)

Snatch tow. A method of recovering a stuck vehicle in which the towing vehicle is in motion before taking up the slack in the tow rope. Use only using special-purpose stretch ropes and specified procedures for this, See 'Recovery – snatch towing', p 86.

Steering lock. The extent to which the steering wheel may be moved to the right or left. Thus 'full lock' implies movement of the steering wheel as far as it will go right or left.

Steering feel. Steering feel is a vital and safety-relevant ingredient of the feedback between vehicle and driver. The communication is achieved almost entirely by assimilating the amount of self-centring or castor action present and how it compares with normal on-road conditions. (See first Castor action and Castor angle above – p 148.) It is important for drivers always to be alert to variations in steering feel and to know what may cause them. A very brief summary follows:
1. *Power steering.* On Land Rover products this is power *assisted* steering so feel is retained at all times. The centre 6°, ie 3° either side of straight ahead, is not power assisted and this aids straight-ahead feel. Be alert to the possibility of inexperienced mechanics having adjusted this out.
2. In *slippery ruts* accurate feel will be lost and you will find it hard to know exactly which way your wheels are pointing. It is essential to check visually until back on normal ground – see p 42, Railway lining effect.
3. In *soft sand*, as noted above, the effective ground contact point may well be ahead of

...continued

Glossary – continued

the pivot axis and this can give 'negative castor action' effect – ie a tendency for the wheels to run away to full lock. This will be particularly – and dangerously – apparent when descending the slip face of a sand dune. Grip the steering wheel firmly with both hands and, down a sandfall, have a marshaller guide you: and watch the marshaller – he is the only one who can tell which way your front wheels are pointing.

4. *Rock or rough ground.* Whilst the worm and roller steering design and power assisted steering of Land Rover vehicles is ideally suited to off-road driving, be aware of the potential for serious kick-back from the steering when traversing rough ground, rocks and boulders. Grip the steering wheel firmly and keep your thumbs outside the rim so that sudden, unexpected kickback does not cause injury.

5. *Range Rover with electronic air suspension.* One of the additional benefits of EAS is that variations in suspension height also cause slight variations in castor angle. Low profile, automatically selected above 50 mph, increases castor angle by just over 1° and produces exceptional stability and enhanced self-centring – exactly what is required for high speed motorway driving. Conversely, when on high profile or extended suspension settings, steering castor is reduced, making the steering inherently lighter over difficult ground.

6. *Ice, snow, slippery conditions* – on road. This will be well-enough known to experienced 4x2 drivers but is still worth mentioning here since the same laws of physics apply to 4x4s. When grip is at a premium obviously the self-centring of the front wheels will be dramatically diminished and the heart-sinking 'lightness' of the steering wheel will be experienced. As in a surprising number of off-road situations, delicate 'finger-tip' steering and 'the midwife's touch' are the order of the day.

Stretch limit (KERR ropes). The extent to which a kinetic energy recovery rope will stretch before it is in danger of breaking. A guide for the Marlow Ropes Recovaline is 40% stretch; this limit should NEVER be approached. See 'Recovery – snatch towing', p 86.

Survey on foot. Inspect before you drive. See On-foot recce above and 'Look before you leap', p 34.

Traction. In the context of this book the concept of achieving grip between the wheels and the ground without slip, skid or sinkage. See pp 12, 28.

Traction Control. See 'Electronic Traction Control, ETC'.

Traction controls. Here taken to mean the lever controlling the transfer gearbox and centre differential lock, see 'Traction controls', p 18.

Tractive effort. The amount of 'pull' exerted by a vehicle as a result of traction.

Trailer preponderance. Sometimes used to denote down-load on the vehicle towing hitch – see 'Nose load' p 155 above and 'Towing – on-road', p 38.

Trailer nose-load. See 'Nose load' p 155 above.

Transfer box. Originally the name implied the transfer of power from the main gearbox to the front axle as well as the rear axle on a four-wheel drive vehicle. In all Land Rover products a two-speed transfer box is fitted so it has the additional role of permitting power from the gearbox to go to the axles at normal 1:1 gearing (high ratio) or geared down by nearly 2:1 (low ratio). See 'Traction – extra gears', p 13, 'Low box – when and how', p 20 and diagram opposite.

Transfer gear lever. The 'small gear lever',

Gearbox, transfer box, hand brake (Early RR shown)

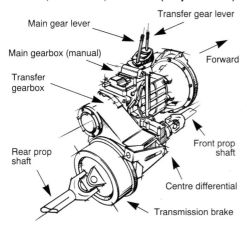

Main gear lever

Transfer gear lever

Main gearbox (manual)

Forward

Transfer gearbox

Rear prop shaft

Front prop shaft

Centre differential

Transmission brake

in the cab next to the main gear lever. It controls whether the transmission is in 'high ratio' or 'low ratio' in the transfer box. The same lever also controls the engagement of the diff lock – see above – except in the Range Rover where a viscous coupling fulfils this requirement automatically. See 'Traction controls', p 18 and 'Viscous coupling', this page.

Transmission brake. The handbrake on all Land Rovers operates by gripping the rear propeller shaft at the point where it leaves the transfer gearbox and is thus called a transmission brake. It should be used as a parking brake only and *should never be operated whilst the vehicle is in motion except in emergency* - see 'Traction controls', p 19 and drawing above.

Transmission wind-up. Read first 'Centre differential', p 149 above. A 4x4 with no centre differential or one driven with the centre diff locked (ie in both cases the front and rear propeller shafts locked together) is unable to accommodate the small differences in distance normally travelled by the front wheels compared to the rear wheels. The diff-lock ensures both propeller shafts rotate exactly the same amount despite the small differences in distance actually travelled. This results in some wheel slip and skid which, on loose

ground, can take place without any harm. On hard roads, however, the superior wheel grip makes it difficult for the wheels to slip much and in the process of trying to do so considerable torsional stress builds up in the transmission. This is known as transmission wind-up and can sometimes exert so much stress that the diff-lock gears will not disengage when so selected. You will also sense very heavy steering. If this occurs due to your forgetting to de-select diff-lock on hard ground (or at any other time) and the diff lock will not disengage, the solution is to reverse the vehicle some distance until the diff-lock warning light extinguishes.

Tyre nomenclature. Details of all information inscribed on the sidewalls of tyres is contained in Section 7, 'Tyres', on p 116 and 117.

Unladen. Vehicle carrying fuel, driver but no payload or other load – see 'Kerb' above.

Unlevelled suspension. Defender 110 rear suspension without the self-levelling option as described at 'Levelled suspension', p 154 above.

Viscous coupling unit (VCU). A unit fitted as standard to all Range Rovers across the centre differential (not instead of it) automatically to effect locking of the differential when a significant speed difference between front and rear propeller shafts is sensed. Conceptually it comprises a cylinder attached to the rear prop shaft

...continued

Glossary – continued

into which an extension of the front prop shaft is introduced. Discs are attached alternately to the front prop shaft and the inside of the cylinder so that they interleave very closely within the cylinder. The cylinder is sealed at both ends and is filled with a special silicone fluid which has the characteristic of markedly *increasing* its viscosity when stirred. Thus when one prop shaft rotates relative to the other one – the situation of front (or rear) axle wheel-spin – the fluid increases its viscosity enough to lock the shafts together. When relative rotation ceases the viscosity changes back to its original value and the shafts are unlocked. The viscous coupling unit (VCU) has the advantage of being automatic on both engagement and disengagement and its action is gradual and without shock-loading to the transmission.

Wading plugs. Oil drain holes are provided in the bottom of the clutch housing (and the camshaft drive-belt housing on Tdi and 2.5D engines) to preclude the possibility of the clutch or cam belts becoming contaminated in the event of oil leaks from the adjacent bearings. Wading plugs should be fitted to block these holes when driving through water over 30 cm deep and subsequently removed. See 'Wading' and photo, p 68.

Wheel-slide. See above 'Discontinuity of rolling contact' p 151. A condition in which one or more wheels slide over a slippery surface rather than rolling over it; can be provoked by brake lock up or excessive engine braking. See 'Gentle right foot', p 28.

Wheel-spin. See Discontinuity of rolling contact p 151. A condition in which a stationary or moving vehicle has power applied to the transmission in conditions of poor grip and one or more wheels spins without associated forward motion (or rearward if in reverse). See 'Gentle right foot', p 28.

GLOSSARY
and
INDEX
section

INDEX

Land Rover Experience

A Defender 110 County on an expedition in the Sahara desert. There are few regions where meticulous vehicle operation and mechanical sympathy could be more important.

Land Rover Experience